STARTING AND MANAGING YOUR POULTRY

Introduction

The course on poultry production seeks to provide you with knowledge on essential building and equipment, incubation of eggs, hatchery management, principles for successful production, breeds and breeding, brooding of chicks and management techniques, how to rear chicks, table egg and meat production, processing and marketing, and products, health management practices, diseases and parasites, and economic implication of these diseases.

Course Objectives

The central objective of this course is to simplify the various components of poultry production in a manner to arouse the interest of the reader(s) in the practical raising of poultry.

After going through this course, you are expected to understand the following:

- The need for poultry building, its features and equipment necessary for raising poultry
- The role of hatchery in modern poultry production
- The different facets in the management of poultry
- How to process poultry meat and egg to meet acceptable standards
- Strategies in marketing of poultry and its products for profitability.

MODULE 1   FACILITIES FOR POULTRY PRODUCTION

Unit 1   Building and Equipment
Unit 2   Incubation
Unit 3   Hatchery Management of Poultry Eggs

UNIT 1   BUILDING AND EQUIPMENT

CONTENTS

1.0   Introduction
2.0   Objectives
3.0   Main Content
    3.1   Definition of Building/Housing
    3.2   Types of Poultry Houses
    3.3   Site Selection and Lay-Out of Poultry Building
    3.4   Features of Poultry Houses
    3.5   Poultry Equipment
        3.5.1 Types of Poultry Equipment
4.0   Conclusion
5.0   Summary
6.0   Assignment
7.0   References

1.0   INTRODUCTION

Generally speaking, the intensification of poultry farming has been towards large commercial flock production. With this trend has come an increase in confinement housing for poultry, hence the investment needs in terms of buildings and equipment. Poultry buildings or constructions entail providing sheds or environment for accommodating birds and store rooms (feeds and equipment). The extent to which these birds are exposed to the environment (sunshine, rain, wind) is determined partly by the system of management and this includes the design of the housing used for birds. Indeed, the birds are unlikely to perform satisfactorily if the housing is poor, therefore correct housing must be provided to meet the optimum requirements for best birds' performance either through growth or egg production. The housing must be suited to the climatic conditions of the environment and poultry houses differ distinctly between the temperate and the tropical countries.

2.0   OBJECTIVES

By the end of this unit you should be able to:

- ensure satisfactory performance of the birds through the provision of adequate housing
- explain the environmental conditions influencing the construction of the poultry houses
- identify and explain the commonly used equipment in poultry production management
- explain what happens when poultry buildings are wrongly sited.

3.0   MAIN CONTENT

3.1   Definition of Building/Housing

These are constructions considered essential to protect the birds from turbulent winds, dust, cold, direct sun light, rain and predators. Buildings are also provided to accommodate feeds and farm equipment. In the tropical environment, an ideal poultry house should not be a completely closed structure. It should be well ventilated, dry cleaned and spacious. It should be of low cost made from locally available building materials.

3.2　　　Types of Poultry Houses

There are many types of houses used by poultry farmers, but only four types that are commonly used shall be discussed here.

1.　　The Full-Sided Wall Poultry House

- This is common in the temperate regions where the temperatures are extremely low.
- In the tropics, this type of house is used for brooding day- old chicks.
- The house is completely insulated by building-up the bricks/blocks to the height of the house.
- Small windows/air spaces are created to allow free flow of air (ventilation).

2.　　The Open-Sided Poultry House

- It is commonly found in the tropical world.

It is recommended that in a hot environment where there is high humidity and temperature, the poultry house should be the open-sided type to allow free flow of air. Floors should be made of concrete. Walls are raised to about 1m high and the remaining upper part of the wall is completed with 1.25cm hexagonal wire mesh. It is used for rearing adult birds. It can be used for younger birds provided the open-sides are covered with plastic or jute materials to conserve heat.

3.　　The Portable Colony Cage

- This type of house is cheap to make. It can be roofed with zinc or asbestos with enough over-hangs to protect rain from splashing into the cages and the sides covered with wire net. In order to ensure coolness at all times, portable colony cages should be placed under shade trees in secured place. A colony cage measuring 4m long, 1.5m wide and 1.8m high can accommodate 60 broilers or 40 layers. If it is made of planks, the wooden legs should be protected against termites and ants.

4.   The Fold Unit

- This is commonly used to house local chickens or chicken reared on the range. It is made of wire mesh just like the two slanting sides. These units are usually placed directly on grassed ground. This enables birds to eat grasses and the unit can be moved from one place to another on regular basis. However there is a great restriction to movement of birds in the fold unit. The fold system also protects young chicks against predators and loss from kites.

3.3   Site Selection and Lay-Out of Poultry Buildings

- This is a very important point to be considered before establishing a commercial poultry farm.
- The sitting of houses should take advantage of topographical features which will favour air movement.
- Records of local wind speeds and direction should be studied to ensure the best orientation to take advantage of prevailing wind i.e. the house should face away from the direction of the prevailing winds and storms in order to avoid rain and wind drought.
- Sites should be planned to avoid obstructions of air movement by other buildings.
- Avoid areas where there is heavy concentration of livestock activity. If this is not possible, choose a place swept by the prevailing winds before the latter reach other farms.
- The best locations are reserved in descending order for: layer breeder stock, future laying pullets, layers and broilers.
    - Avoid sites prone to water logging; houses must be on a ground high enough to provide drainage and should be protected against the danger of floods, i.e. they should be located on well-drained sites.
    - The site should be accessible from an all season; motorable roads to enhance delivery of feeds; removal of poultry products and wastes.
    - A steady source of water and electricity should also be considered.

3.4   Features of Poultry Houses

For poultry farmers constructing housing under tropical environmental conditions, certain requirements must be met if the house is to provide an adequate environment. Considerations for the following factors will avoid pit falls later.

1.   **Foundation of House:** A solid and strong foundation is necessary to support the building.

- Digging should be done to a depth of between 0.5 to 0.7m or more depending on the nature of soil.
- After digging, a layer of concrete should be poured into a depth of about 10cm; this will form the basement upon which the blocks will be laid.
- To minimize the effect of termites, an anti-termite chemical (solignum) can be poured on top of this basement.
- Before building up the rest of the foundation, provision should be made for the erection of pillars at intervals along the length of the building. These pillars will support the roof in an open-sided poultry house.
- Floor of house: The floor should be thick enough to give protection against wetness or dampness during the wet season.
- Concrete floor is mandatory for deep litter system of management especially when the soil is very dense and can absorb and transfer moisture from the lower subsoil.
- Rammed laterite after sand filling may work well, but in such a case, the floor should be raised at least 30cm above the outside ground level, depending on the water level.
- The floor should be cemented to make it easy to clean and wash.
- Concrete floor control rat problems in poultry houses.

2.   **Width of House:** The width from front to back of the open-sided

poultry house could be up to 10m (36 ft) in order to ensure effective natural ventilation.

- Houses that are wider than this may not provide ample ventilation during the dry season.
  - This recommended width is basic for growing birds, broilers or for laying hens.

- The houses could be made wider if ceiling fans or air conditioners are installed.

3. **Length of House:** A poultry house may be almost of any convenient length.

- The terrain on which the house is to be built often determines the length.
- Maximum length of 120metres is acceptable
- When automatic feeding equipment is to be installed, this will limit the length of the poultry house.
- Therefore the equipment manufacturer should be consulted about the length of chain and the gears of the automatic feeder before length of the building is determined.

4. **Wall of House:** The walls may be built up with cement or mud blocks.

- The walls can vary from full walls with windows to almost no wall at all i.e. dwarf walls.
- The same open-sided house suitable for adult birds may be adapted for brooding chicks by covering the open sides with plastic sheets to conserve heat for the young birds during these first few weeks of life.
- If it is be to open-sided, provision should be made for the erection of pillars at 1.3 to 1.6m (4-5ft) apart.
- Wooden pillars are good enough but may need to be partially re-enforced with concrete up to the length of the solid portion of the wall.
- The solid portion of the wall should be one-third (0.8 – 1m) to half of the total height of the wall/stud (2.4 -3m) high. The stud represents the distance from the foundation to the roof line, topped by 0.9 -1.6m wide strip of $1/2$inch chicken wire mesh.
- If battery cages are to be used for growers or layers, the solid walls should be less than 0.8m.

5. **Roof of House:** The roof of a poultry house may be full-span (gable) or lean-to

- Gable poultry houses built today have gable roof.
- Gable roof structure with ridge ventilation provides excellent ventilation.
- The height of the ridge is related to the width of the house,
- The difference between the ridge and eave heights is about one quarter of the width of the house for houses of 7.2m or less in width.
- Lean- to roofs may create the problem of rain drifting into the house.

- With all types of roofs it is important to provide a good roof– overhang of about 0.9m (3ft). This is necessary to prevent rain from entering the house through the open sides of the wall.
- The over hang may be longer on the side of the building facing the rain bearing wind.
- Higher roof tend to make the house cooler especially where a ceiling is not provided.
- Roofing materials such as corrugated asbestos, corrugated iron sheets or aluminum sheets with hardwood supports are durable and will last longer than thatched roof but they cost more.
- Iron sheets increase temperatures inside the house during the hot months of the year unless plenty of shade trees are presented-insulator against heat figure.

6. Doors of house should be wide enough; not less than 0.9m

- This is to facilitate easy movement of staff, equipment, birds and manure in and out of the house after depopulation.
- A footbath/depression at the door step is needed at the foot of each door.
- The footbath may be built in at the doorstep or it may be in a movable container.

7. **Storage Space:** A store may be situated at the middle of the house, but should preferably be a separate building.

- There should be two stores: one for eggs, the other for feed and other items needed for farm operation.
- The size of such a space should be about one-tenth of the total size of the house.

Gabble roof type with ridge opening

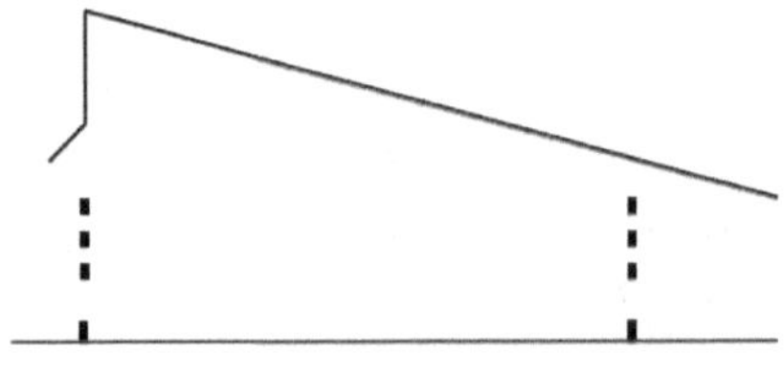

Lean – to roof type

3.5 Poultry Equipment

Poultry equipment is made up of instruments or tools used for a particular job or activity in poultry production management.

Poultry houses can not function satisfactorily unless they are properly equipped and supplied with appliances. These are the basic requirements for the successful management of fowls. Poultry equipment vary from the simple to the complex and from the most elementary to the most advanced electronic devices.

Poultry equipment can be broadly grouped into those for general applications and those for specific applications. Those for general applications are used at all post- natal stages of growth; these consist mainly of feeders, drinkers and crates. Those for specific stages of growth include brooders for chicks-brooding and nests for layers.

3.5.1 Types of Poultry Equipment

1.   **Feeders**

- Feeders are appliances used to supply feed to the birds.
- The construction of feeders should be such as to avoid waste, to prevent fouling of feed with droppings and litter, to facilitate cleaning or washing and should be constructed from durable materials.
- If timber is used for construction, preservatives like solignum should be used to prevent fungal or insect-damage.
- Feeders are mostly troughs or hoppers.
- The trough feeder comes in a variety of sizes and designs.
- The length can be about 0.6m to 1.6m
- The base width of a sloping-sided trough is about 5-8cm when the trough is for 8-week-old birds and 20-25cm for adult.
- The feeders could have legs which lift them above the litter.
- The top of each of the long sides is curved in to form a "lip" as a means of limiting feed waste.

  - A spinner mounted on top of the feeder gives sufficient access to feed and prevent fouling and wastage of feed by the bird.

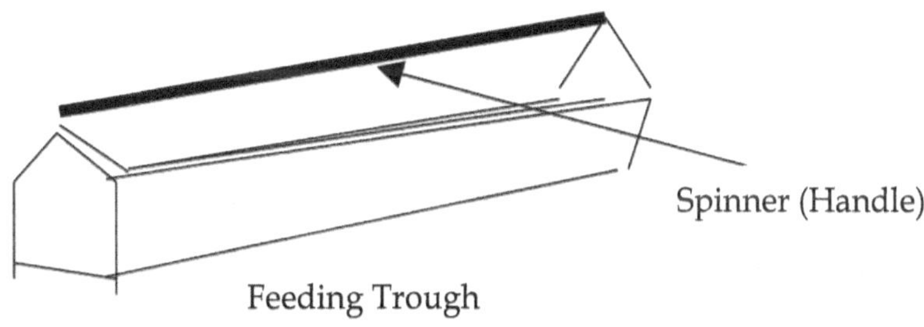

Tube feeders or hanging feeders: These are metal feeders which are cylindrical in shape, and with a pin into which feed flows from the main body in which reserve feed is contained.

- They vary from about 6kg to 14kg in the quantities of feed that they can hold.

  - Height of feeder should always be set level with the back of the bird.
  - Some of them have covers at the top end.
  - Another type of tube feeder has sloping sides, wider at the base than at the top.
  - Automatic feeders may become important with the increasing cost of labour in many tropical areas.
  - One form distributes feed from the feed-hopper through a chain that is electrically driven and operated by a time switch.
  - It activates feed and reduces crowding but it is expensive.

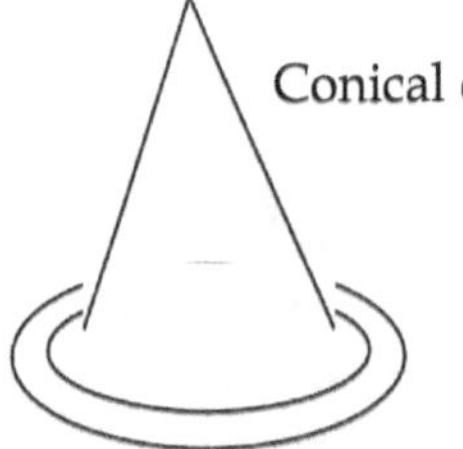

Conical drinkers

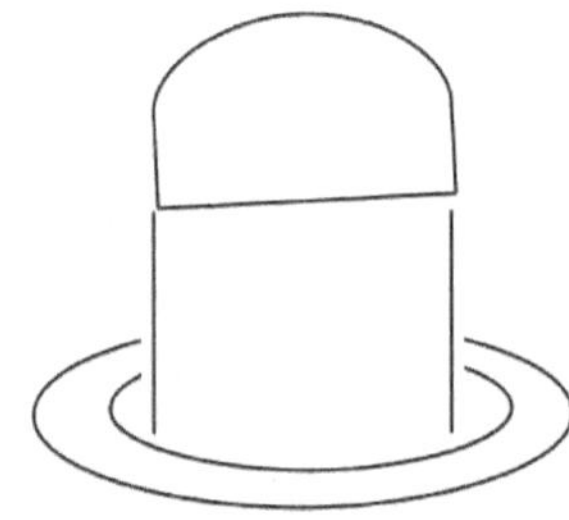

2.   Drinkers

The commonest form of drinker in Nigeria is the water fountain, which may be made of galvanized iron, aluminum, plastic or clay.

- They are usually conical or partly cylindricated.
- They vary in capacity from 2 to 6 or 8 litres.
- The shape should facilitate quick and thorough washing.
- Some drinkers are trough-shaped.

- They are made of galvanized angle iron.
- Bars spaced at 7.5cm prevent fouling of the water.
- The trough may be filled manually or by an automatic device based on a spring-loaded ball-valve attached to the supply pipe.
- The base of the drinker should have a groove that controls the water flow to the surrounding.

3.   Perch

This equipment is necessary in deep litter houses.

- It provides resting or roosting places
- It is made of metal, wood, or plastic
- It is of moderate height, to minimize egg breakages.

4. Nests

- This equipment is peculiar to the management of layers and breeders.
- Nests are compartments in which eggs are laid.
- The compartments may be such that can be used by one or more birds at a time.
- Some nests are single or open-fronted nests where dimensions are 25-30cm wide, 30-35cm high and 30 -36 cm deep.
- There is a 1.5-10cm litter-retaining board across the front.
- There is also an alighting perch 10cm from where the birds can alight before entering the nest.
- Ideally there should be a means for closing the nests in the evening so that birds don't roost in and dirty eggs.
- Two types of nest boxes could be used; they are individual nest boxes and colony nest boxes.
- Nests could be arranged in 2-3 tiers, each having four to six nests. The lowest tier could be about 45cm off the floor.
- Nests are usually built with a light frame work covered with cardboard or are of metal construction.
- The floor of the nest and possibly a section of the side may be constructed with wire mesh.
- The top should be slopping so that fowls may not roost on the nests.
- Nests could vary from just a dark corner cordoned off by a few bricks, wood, ceiling board, old basket, old boxes or-purposed built nests.
- The floor of the nest should have litter material to provide a cushion effect on the egg and reduce breakages.

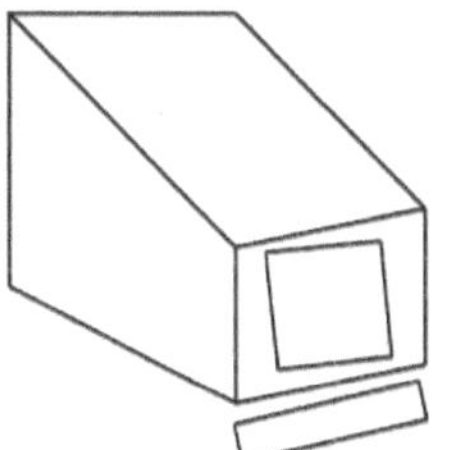

The single laying nest

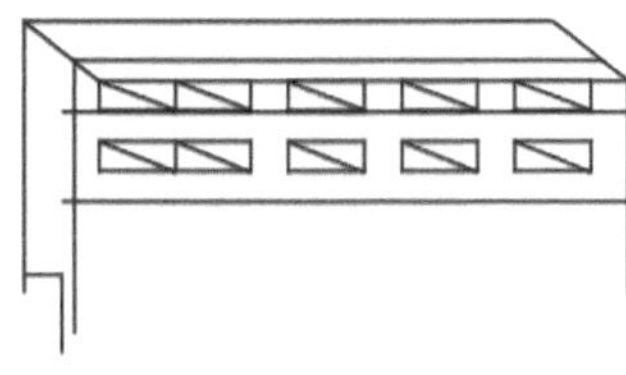

The two-tier single nest

5. Crates

These are perforated or well ventilated boxes for the transfer of adult fowls and sometimes growers.

- The crates could be made of light wood or plastic. framework on iron.
- They could be used to convey 15-25 birds at a time depending on their age and size.
- Corners of crate should not be sharp, prevent pilling and suffocation.

6. Tools

It is good to be well equipped with tools because it encourages "do it yourself" attitude, which encourages innovation and self relevance. Example: pliers, shovels, wheel barrow, cutlasses, holes, rakes, hammer, saw, screw drivers, scoops, etc.

7. Brooders

Brooders provide heat for young birds for the first few weeks of life during which they are unable to regulate their own body temperature.

- Brooder guards restrict the young birds to within the vicinity of heat and feed supply.
- Brooder guards can be made from flexible materials such as ceiling boards cardboard or wire netting.
- Brooder types Vent for the exit of hot air kerosene lamp or stoves, electricity heaters or bulbs and brooder hens.

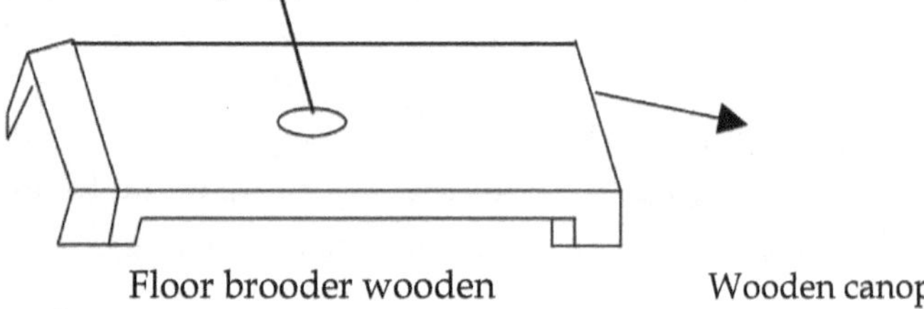

Floor brooder wooden   Wooden canopy

4.0 CONCLUSION

Adequate poultry housing is needed to protect birds from rain, direct sunlight, heat, cold, turbulent winds, dust etc. In the tropical environment, an ideal poultry house should be well ventilated, dry, clean and spacious. It should be accessible for good patronage. Finally, poultry houses cannot function satisfactorily unless they are properly equipped and supplied with appliances.

5.0 SUMMARY

In this unit, we have been able to delve into the essentials of poultry buildings as they relate to housing of birds and equipment. Considerable factors for sitting and laying out of buildings to avoid pit falls later were equally addressed. Also, different types of houses and equipment for operational activities in a poultry production management system have been explained.

6.0 ASSIGNMENT

1. What are the pre-requisites for sitting a poultry house?
2. List the specific and non-specific poultry equipment.
3. Define poultry equipment.
4. What are the different types of poultry houses?
5. List the features of a poultry house.

7.0 REFERENCES

Oluyemi, J. A. and Roberts, F.A. (2000). *Poultry Production in Warm Wet Climates*. London: Macmillan Publishers Ltd. Pp. 58 – 86.

Ganiyu, O. (2005). *Poultry Care: A Complete Guide to Chicken Production*. Ganob and Associates Ltd. Pp. 10 – 18.

UNIT 2   INCUBATION

CONTENTS

1.0   Introduction
2.0   Objectives
3.0   Main Content
        3.1   The Background of Incubation
        3.2   Incubators
                3.2.1 Differences between the Two Types of
                Incubators
        3.2.2 Incubation Periods of the Eggs of Various Birds
                3.2.3 Incubation Practices
                        3.2.3.1 The Incubation Environment

        3.2.4 Other Management Practices on Fertile Eggs in the
                Incubator
        3.2.5 Causes of Embryonic
        Death
4.0   Conclusion
5.0   Summary
6.0   Tutor-Marked Assignment
7.0   References/Further Readings

1.0   INTRODUCTION

Incubation is described as the management of a fertilized egg to ensure the satisfactory development of the embryo inside into a normal chick or poult or keet.

Incubation may be achieved by the natural method with a hen sitting on the eggs, or artificially by using special machines called incubators. The incubators are placed in specially constructed buildings known as hatcheries. Artificial incubation refers to the use of mechanical equipment to replace a brooding hen for the incubation of eggs. The use of incubators has freed the breeding hen from incubating eggs and enables her to work "full-time" during the year to reproduce fertile eggs. This is because the reproductive capacity of the hen could not be used or attained without artificial incubation of eggs. The development of the incubator is the foundation of the modern poultry industry allowing large numbers of newly hatched chicks to be produced on demand by the poultry producers. The production of fertile eggs that will produce strong viable chicks is the key factor in a successful hatchery operation.

2.0   OBJECTIVES

At the end of this unit, you should be able to:

- give the reasons for the development of the incubator and its functions
- highlight the general practices in an incubator
- explain how to manage fertile eggs in the incubator.

3.0   MAIN CONTENT

3.1   The Background of Incubation

Artificial incubation is an ancient occupation. Both the Chinese and the Egyptians are credited with originating artificial incubation procedures as far back as 300 B.C. and 500 B.C, respectively. Early incubation in both countries was very similar and it was believed they had the same origin. However, over the years, the incubation process has become a very sophisticated one; incubators have been developed and refined to the point where they are almost completely automatic (such as having automatic turning devices, thermostats to regulate temperature, humidly and air exchange).

3.2   Incubators

These are machines that are manufactured to artificially provide heat in place of a brooder hen to ensure the satisfactory management of a fertilized egg to produce normal chick or poult or keet. The incubator is either a table type (i.e. flat and natural draught) or cabinet type (i.e. forced-draught). Both types are essentially insulated chambers in which temperature and relative humidity are controlled. However, most of the new ones are forced- draught: that is they have fans to circulate the air. They are capable of maintaining more even temperature, full, and oxygen levels than steam air. Today commercial incubators vary in capacity from a few thousand to many thousands of eggs. The table has a small capacity, between 50-450 eggs. Many modern commercial hatcheries also use separate setter and hatcher machines, which can be placed in separate rooms, thus minimizing the transfer of disease among eggs. Also, the hatcher can be fumigated more frequently or often, as there is no risk of contaminating the eggs in the setter with the chemicals.

3.2.1 The Differences between Flat and Cabinet Incubators

- Eggs are trayed vertically, broad end up in a cabinet incubator but horizontally in a flat type.
- Eggs are tilted through 90_o-45_o to each sides of the vertical axis in cabinet incubator as opposed to being rolled through 180 in a flat type.
- Ventilation is mechanically assisted in a cabinet incubator and natural draught supplied in the flat.
- The flat type takes only a few eggs of between 50-500 and is meant for the small scale producer while the cabinet is used in commercial hatcheries.

3.2.2 Incubation Periods of the Eggs of Various Birds

Different species of birds and even the strains of birds lay eggs that have different incubation periods. Although some species have the same period of incubation, most do not have the same. So whether it is natural or artificial incubation that is used, the eggs must stay in the incubator for the required period of time before they are finally hatched into chicks or poults.

These incubation periods can only be kept strictly when conditions within and outside the incubators are favorable for the eggs. Under certain situations even after the period is elapsed the chicks or poults are not hatched and when they eventually hatch, hatchability is very low. Examples of incubation period of eggs of various birds:

Species	Days
Bob white quail, pheasants	24

Japanese quail, pigeons	16-19
Chickens	21- 22
Duck (muscovy), swan	35
Ostrich	42
Canary	13
Duck (Pekin and mallard), goose,	28
Guinea fowl and turkey	

3.2.3 Incubation Practices

The success of incubation practices starts with the quality of eggs via the breeding stock. The breeder flock must be healthy and free of all pathogens. Hatchable eggs meant for setting in the incubator should be handled with utmost care. Fertile eggs should be collected at least three times a day. This is necessary to ensure that they are not soiled and can be cooled faster. Misshapen size, thin or cracked shells or those that are excessively big should be rejected. The eggs weighing 55–60 grams are ideal for hatching. Once they are selected, they should be fumigated with a suitable agent such as formaldehyde, dried, cleaned or dipped or washed in warm sanitizing agent.

3.2.3.1   The Incubation Environment/Environmental Conditions inside the Incubator

For successful artificial incubation, there are certain elements in the atmosphere which are conductive to incubation that need to be provided for efficient functioning of the incubator. The modern incubator is designed to operate within specific limits of an environment where temperature, humidity and air flow are controlled.

1.   Incubator Room Temperature

Embryonic development is initiated when the egg is exposed to a temperature of 26.6 – 29.4^{0}C but development is most satisfactory when the temperature ranges from 32.2 - 39.4$_0$C. Within a moderate range, incubator temperature directly influences the rate of embryonic development. If relatively low, it leads to delayed hatching and if high, it hastens hatching. High incubator temperature may cause unhealed navels, thereby assisting the entry of bacterial infection. Excessively high or low temperature causes death of embryo at any stage of incubation. The optimum recommended dry bulb temperature is 37.6 + 0.2^{0}C for the first 18 days of incubation. Under practical conditions the wet bulb thermometer should read 30$_0$C in the incubator.

2. Relative Humidity

Relative humidity is of great importance for a developing embryo. As the embryo grows, it losses moisture through the shell of the eggs, which must be regulated for the healthy chick to hatch. A lower level of moisture in the chamber increases the weight loss while the higher level reduces it. Availability of optimum level of moisture in the incubation chamber stimulates the growth of the embryo. The moisture loss from the eggs depend on the porosity of the shell and size of eggs. The average weight loss of egg during the 19 days of incubation should be 10 to 11% under the normal recommended level of relative humidity i.e. 55 – 60%.

3. Ventilation

Ventilation is the process of changing bad air from the incubators, in this case, with fresh air. It can be achieved by natural or mechanical means depending on the capacity and type of incubator. The developing embryo from an average egg size of 58g respires by consuming 5.11_3 of oxygen and emits 2.81^3 of carbon dioxide throughout the incubation period. Oxygen starvation results in reduced survival of embryo and low hatchability. The best oxygen concentration in incubator is 21%. The optimum level of carbon dioxide in the incubator is 0.5% with a range of 0.4 to 0.6%. Ventilation is needed to rid the incubator of ammonia and other noxious substances arising perhaps from the spoilage of some eggs.

3.2.4 Other Management Practices in the Incubator

1. Egg Selection

Eggs that weigh between 55–60 grams are selected for incubation to avoid an uneven distribution of heat, relative humidity and oxygen.

2. Candling

Candling is a process of examining fertile eggs against a strong beam of light preferably emerging through a small hole or a narrow slit. The test is conducted in a dark room. In this process the light reaches the eye of the observer after passing through the egg, thereby making the content fairly visible. This test may be conducted at 5_{th} to 7_{th} day and 18_{th} day of incubation, in order to eliminate the infertile or clear eggs at the early stage of embryonic growth and the dead in shell later in life.

3.   **Turning**

Turning of the eggs during the incubation process is absolutely necessary in order to prevent adhering of the embryos to the shell membranes during the early stages of development. It also helps in providing uniform environment for the incubating eggs and the growing embryos. Depending on the type and capacity of the incubator, the eggs may be turned manually or mechanically at regular intervals of 5 to 7 times a day. The eggs must rest between turnings. Constant back and forth motion is bad for the hatch. The turning angle should be at least 45_0.

4.   **Positioning of Eggs**

The positioning of eggs in the incubator is one of the factors affecting hatchability. The eggs are positioned in the incubator such that the broad ends are up. Eggs with narrow ends up show unduly high proportion of dead in shell through the failure of the embryo's head to establish access air space, thus hatchability will reduce by 30–40%.

3.2.5 Causes of Embryo Death

Certain features are usually associated with the different causes of embryonic mortality or poor management operations:

1.   Failure to hatch following piping may be due to insufficient moisture.
2.   Hatching too soon and malformed chicks may arise from excessively high temperature.
3.   Weak chicks may result from overheating of the incubator.

4. "Mushy" chicks may be caused by too low an average temperature and poor ventilation of incubator; the chicks get weak, drowsy and puffed up and death occurs shortly.

5. Blood rings in broken-out shells suggest early embryonic death and may be due to either high or too low an incubator temperature, incorrect fumigation or wrong storage of eggs.

4.0   CONCLUSION

The aim of incubation is to ensure the satisfactory development of fertilized eggs either naturally or artificially into normal chicks. This unit explains the management of environmental factors that can affect the successful development of the embryo in an incubator. It also shows that the quality of the hatch is also dependent on turning, candling and positioning of eggs in the incubator.

5.0   SUMMARY

In this unit you have been introduced to the concept of incubation, types of incubators and the differences between them. Successful artificial incubation depends on the incubator environment, the quality of the eggs and other management practices in the incubator. You have also been introduced to the features that are likely to be associated with different causes of embryonic mortality.

6.0   ASSIGNMENT

1. What is incubation?
2. Differentiate between the flat and cabinet incubator.
3. Briefly explain the environmental conditions that will encourage good embryo development.
4. Of what importance is the incubator to the poultry industry?
5. What is the incubation period of eggs of these species of poultry?

    (a)   Chicken   (b)   Ostrich   (c)   Bobwhite quail
    (d)   Turkey   (e)   Swan

7.0   REFERENCES

Adeyinka, I. A. and Auta, J. H. (2002). *Incubation and Hatchery Practices: Poultry Production in Nigeria*. A Training Manual for National Training Workshop: NAPRI, Shika, Nigeria PP. 54 – 68.

Oluyemi, J. A. and Roberts, F. A. (2000). *Poultry Production in Warm Wet Climates*. Ibadan: Spectrum Books Ltd.

Saxena, H.C. and Ketelaars, E. H. (1993). *Poultry Production in Hot Climate Zones*. New Delhi: Kalyani Publishers,

UNIT 3   HATCHERY MANAGEMENT OF POULTRY EGGS

CONTENTS

1.0   Introduction
2.0   Objectives
3.0   Main Content
    3.1   Hatchery Practices
        3.1.1 Hatchery Hygiene

        3.1.2 Factors Required for Maintaining Proper Hatchery Hygiene
        3.1.3 Factors   Influencing   Successful   Hatchery

Operation
s
3.2   Sitting of Hatchery
        Hatchery
3.3   Building
3.4   Handling of Hatchery Eggs
        Management of Hatchery Eggs in the
3.5   Hatcher
3.6   Providing the Best Hatchery Environment
        3.6.1   Temperature
        3.6.2   Relative Humidity
                Ventilatio
        3.6.3   n
        3.6.4   Turning of Eggs
        3.6.5   Position of the Eggs
4.0   Conclusion
5.0   Summary
6.0   Tutor-Marked Assignment
7.0   References/Further Resources

1.0   INTRODUCTION

A hatchery is a place where eggs are hatched into chicks, poults or keet by artificial means (incubator). The hatching of chicks as a business has long been an important part of the poultry industry in the whole world. Hatchery management begins even before the eggs to be hatched arrive at the hatchery. It involves the location of the hatchery, the type of equipment and the skilled labour necessary in the hatchery etc. The hatchery manager must know exactly what kinds of material are being put into the setters. The actual process of hatching a chick is complicated as there are many factors affecting it. The environment in which the eggs are incubated and the environmental factors in the setters and hatchery provide the proper conditions for embryo development. If the hatchery is not performing up to the hatchability standard recommended by the breeder supplier, there is a probability that inadequate ventilation could be the problem.

2.0   OBJECTIVES

At the end of this unit, you should be able to:

- advice an industrious farmer where to locate a hatchery
- highlight the pertinent requirement for successful hatchery operations
- describe how a hatchery environment can be controlled for better hatchability.

3.0   MAIN CONTENT

3.1   Hatchery Practices

It should be noted that the health status of the breeding flock is very important for the production of high quality hatchery eggs. Also important in this regard is the mating ratio which is usually 6–7 males to 100 females for the commercial egg production breeder and 7–9 males per 100 females for broiler breeders. The most decisive factor towards achieving optimum results is good management. The precise information that the hatchery manager requires for successful hatchery practices includes: the health and age of breeders (parent flock), vaccination status, stocking ratio, fumigation program of the eggs and hatchery equipment and lastly interval between egg collection and setting.

3.1.1 Hatchery Hygiene

The hatchery is the greatest potential source for the spread of diseases within the poultry industry. The problem usually starts with contaminated eggs which are incubated under ideal conditions for microbiological reproduction. The infection passes to the hatched chick and can then be disseminated.

There are some obvious factors which not only result in a large number of hatcheries becoming contaminated and infected but also magnify the risks and render it difficult to eliminate the infection, if it is established. Eggs supplied to a hatchery could come from many flock farms with birds of differing age, health and production status.

Hatchery business is a continuous process. Setters are rarely emptied, and one egg explosion can contaminate hundreds or even thousands of eggs around it. Hatchery fluff can contain up to 10,000,000 organisms/gm. Since the quality of the out put has a direct relationship with input management starts with successful egg management.

3.1.2 Factors Required for Maintaining Proper Hatchery Hygiene

1.   Handling of Fertile Eggs

Apart from the congenital infection, eggs are normally bacteriologically sterile when they are laid. Any contamination of the eggs which occur is picked up from the external environment between laying and hatching. Eggs are particularly susceptible to infection during the first few hours after laying when they are cooling down. Micro-organisms picked up on the surface of the shell can quickly penetrate them. Because of this, the environment from the nest box onwards is very crucial. Nests must therefore be supplied with fresh litter material to keep the eggs as clean as possible.

The following steps will ensure a reduction of contaminants on the fertile eggs:

- Collect eggs frequently – fertile eggs should be collected 4 to 5 times a day.

2.   Fumigate the Eggs

Do this with para-formaldehyde within 4 hours of laying on the farms; special cabinets and mini fumigators are available for this purpose. Ideally dirty eggs should not be passed into the hatchery. These eggs are sometimes subjected to varying treatments including ineffective washing which has a disastrous effect on chick quality. After fumigation eggs must be stored and transported to the hatchery in boxes, trays, trolleys and vehicles which must have been previously sanitized with a heavy duty detergent sanitizer. If possible discard fibre trays after using once, otherwise ensure they are thoroughly fumigated.

3.   Ensure that the Setter is Clean

Multi-stage setters are usually frequently cleaned and sanitized since they are not emptied for a period of up to two years. In an attempt to control the build up and transfer of infection from exploding eggs, fogging with disinfectants is a standard practice. Many of the products used for fogging setters are embryocidal and have a very adverse effect on hatchability. Avoid fumigation of eggs in the setters from 24 to 96 hours after setting. Soak setter trays between uses in a pressure washer. Scrub setter room floor twice a week using a suitable disinfectant.

4. Use Appropriate Detergent Sanitizer to Clean the Hatchers

To reduce the number of micro-organisms in the lime scale, on the floors and walls of the hatchers as well as the trolleys and other equipment to an acceptable level of $100/16cm^2$, it is vital that the detergent sanitizer used is capable of penetrating any lime-scale building and destroying the organisms present.

5. Carry out Aerial Disinfection

Many hatcheries fog the total hatchery environment on a daily basis. The products used vary from formalin to pine-disinfectants. Quaternary ammonium type disinfectant is very suitable.

6. Other General Factors

- All employees should wash hands frequently especially between operations. Provide wash hands basins, germicidal soap and paper towels.
- Protective clothing should not be damaged between operations.
- Avoid staff movement within the hatchery. Under no circumstances should, a staff move from the hatchery room to the egg handling room.
- During candling and transfer, any broken eggs or exploded eggs should be immediately placed in a container of disinfectant and completely submerged. The area should be fogged following such an explosion.
- The collection vehicle and chick transporters should be cleaned regularly and fumigated.
- At all costs prevent back tracking in the hatchery. Keep doors closed at all times, by the use of automatic devices.
- Routine bacterial monitoring should be undertaken to check overall hygiene.

3.1.3 Factors Influencing Successful Hatchery Operations, Management of Breeder Flock and Hatching of Eggs

1. **Diet and Health Status of Flock:** The breeder hen must be kepthealthy and provided with a diet adequate to supply the fertile egg with all nutrients necessary, not only for normal embryonic development, but also to maintain the offspring in healthy conditions until it consumes adequate feed. It bears emphasis here that the quality of a breeder ration is more than for the laying ration.

2. **A Healthy Breeder Flock is the Best Insurance for Good Quality Offerings:** Breeder hens that are in poor health for any reason frequently either fail to supply the embryo with some vital nutritional

factors or perhaps pass some toxins to the eggs, thus, the hatch is poor or the chicks are of poor quality and must be culled.

3. **Preventing Interior Egg Borne Disease:** Various techniques are used for preventing disease agents from being carried to the offspring. The ideal situation is to have breeders free of all pathogens. Such procedures include: immunization during the growing period to prevent infection and egg transmission during the laying period (e.g. avian encephalomyelities, (CRD), tests and removal of carriers or slaughter of infected locks (e.g. pullorum and fowl typhoid).

4. **Preventing Egg Shell** – borne diseases: Several procedures are used to overcome shell contamination which arises from intestinal contents and other environmental sources. Control involves preventing shell contamination or destroying the organisms before they penetrate the shell. This could be achieved through:

   - Producing clean hatching eggs
   - Fumigation
   - Washing in water of 38ºC or liquid sterilization (sodium pentachlorophenate).

3.2 Sitting of Hatchery

It is fundamental that the hatchery should be located away from existing farms, farm houses and densely populated areas/human settlements. There should be easy supply of electricity, hygienic water and open air. Hatchery must be well connected with the roads and egg production centres. The immediate surrounding of the hatchery should be properly cleaned and kept hygienic at all times. Hatchery waste should be properly disposed of and the equipment sanitized.

3.3 The Hatchery Building

The dimensions of the hatchery building will depend on the number and size of the machine to be accommodated, which in turn will depend on the number of chicks required to be hatched in a given period of time. The lay out plan, however, must meet basic hatchery premises plan.

1. **The Egg Receiving Room**

   It should be located at the outset of hatchery premises. The eggs from breeder farm may be received here preferably through the window and the person bringing them should not be allowed to enter the hatchery building.

2.   The Disinfection, Fumigation and Holding Room

Fumigation room should be connected to the egg receiving room and after disinfection/fumigation eggs may be shifted to the cold storage/holding room.The egg holding room should be connected to the fumigation room.

3.   The Egg Setting Room

This should be quite spacious so that sufficient working space furnished with work benches etc. are available for the workers to do the job effectively, besides accommodating the required number of incubators.

4.   The Candling Room

Evidently, the candling chamber should be dark and connected to the egg setting as well as hatching rooms. It should be equipped with fertility testing lamps or mass candler. The eggs are candled for internal egg quality prior to loading in the incubators located in the setting room.

5.   The Hatching Room

Hatchers should preferably be kept in a separate room. This part of the building should specifically be ideally cleaned and well ventilated for the production of large numbers of healthy chicks.

6.   The Chick Sexing Room

This room may be attached to hatching room as well as the chick holding room. The room should be clubbed with appropriate light source (200-watt electric bulb in a reflector is essential) for chick sexing.

7.   The Chick Holding and Supply Room

8.   The Store/Office

A hatchery plan – natural ventilation

3.4   **Storage Temperature of Hatchable Eggs**

To enhance proper hatchability, it is generally recommended that hatchable eggs should be stored in air conditioned room at a temperature range of between 13–16^{0}C and a relative humidity of 75–80%, and shouldn't be stored longer than seven days, but preferably four days. The large end of the eggs must be held up and the position should be changed daily to reduce embryonic abnormalities.

3.5   Management of Hatchable Eggs in the Hatcher

After candling on the 18th day (three days to hatching for other species), the entire healthy embryo should be shifted on the 19$_{th}$ day to the hatching compartment very gently without exposing the eggs to the outside environment for a longer period. The following are some management tips to enhance a good hatch.

3.6 Providing the Best Hatching Environment

3.6.1 Temperature

The temperature on the 20th and 21st day should be between 27.2^{0}C– 36.1$_0$C in the hatching compartment. The thermometers should be checked occasionally for accuracy.

3.6.2 Relative Humidity

During this time humidity must be increased to about 75% to achieve the following:

- Help the chicks break through the shell membrane
- Prevent the beak of the chicks from sticking to the shell and
- Stop the chick from drying out.

3.6.3 Ventilation

Only through trial and error can the correct amount of ventilation be determined through experimentation. The following are some helpful figures:

- In the hatcher 0.6–1.0% CO_2 and 20–21% O_2
- In the room 0.04–0.05% CO_2 and 20.8%-21% O_2

3.6.4 Turning of Eggs

In the hatcher, the eggs are not turned in order to avoid any disturbance to the growing chick.

3.6.5 Position of the Eggs

The eggs should be trayed with the large end up because, in nature, the head of the chick develops in the large end of the egg near the air cell. The reversed positioning will reduce hatchability by 30–40%.

4.0   CONCLUSION

The success of any hatchery operation depends on several factors ranging from what happens on the breeder farm to what finally happens in the hatchery. Thus attempts must be made in examining some of the important steps involved in incubation and hatchery operations in order to achieve good hatchability.

5.0   SUMMARY

In this unit, we have examined the hatchery management practices that will enhance successful hatchability, sitting of hatchery and the lay out plan of hatchery buildings. We also discussed handling and management of hatchable eggs in the hatcher.

6.0   ASSIGNMENT

1.   Sketch the plan of a hatchery
2.   List the required factors in maintaining proper hatchery hygiene.
3.   What are the factors affecting hatchability?

MODULE 2 FUNDAMENTALS FOR SUCCESSFUL POULTRY PRODUCTION

Unit 1 Principles for Successful Poultry Production
Unit 2 Nutrient Requirements of Poultry
Unit 3 Breeds and Breeding

UNIT 1 PRINCIPLES FOR SUCCESSFUL POULTRY PRODUCTION

CONTENTS

  Introductio
1.0 n
2.0 Objectives
  Main
3.0 Content
  3.1 Feeds and Feeding in Poultry Production
    3.1.1 Definition of Terms
  3.2 Classification of Feed Ingredients
    3.2.1 Carbohydrates
    3.2.2 Protein
    3.2.3 Fats
    3.2.4 Minerals
    3.2.5 Vitamins
    3.2.6 Water
  3.3 Anti Nutritional Factors
  3.4 Feeding Practices
    3.4.1 Feed Presentation
      3.4.1.1 The Unrestricted Feeding Programme
      3.4.1.2 The Restricted Feeding Programme
    3.4.2 Forms of Feeds
  3.5 Tips to Achieving High Feed Efficiency
4.0 Conclusion
5.0 Summary
6.0 Assignment
7.0 References

1.0 INTRODUCTION

The transformation of plants, animals and mineral matters into forms highly prized as a source of food for man is the primary basis for the poultry industry. From the nutritional stand point, the nutrients contained in a poultry feed are as useful to man as to a laying hen. However, as eggs or poultry meat, these nutrients are in a much more palatable form. For profitable poultry production, the conversion of feed to eggs and meat must be done efficiently and economically. To formulate rations that will do this, it is necessary to know something of the food nutrients and their use by the poultry.

2.0   OBJECTIVES

At the end of this unit you should be able to:

- explain the basic principles of feeds and feeding
- state briefly the purpose of feeding
- select feed ingredients to compound diets for poultry
- outline the forms of feed presentation to poultry.

3.0   MAIN CONTENT

3.1   Feeds and Feedings in Poultry Production

Poultry feeding is a major item of cost in poultry production. It is estimated to account for between 60 to 80 per cent of the total cost of producing eggs and poultry meat.

Adequate nutrition is essential in profitable chicken production enterprises. When chickens are provided with high quality feed at the required quantity, it promotes body maintenance, growth, improves egg production, and it gives energy, good health and vigour.

Maintenance of the body is the first consideration in good feeding. Under normal conditions, production follows after the body needs are supplied. Considerable feed is required to build and maintain the body to the point of production. Actual production of eggs requires but a comparatively small amount of food in addition. Profit comes from growth or production of meat or eggs. About three -fourth of the total feed consumed is used for maintenance when a fowl is in laying condition.

3.1.1 Definition of Terms

There are a number of terms which should be defined before the principles of feeding are discussed further.

Nutrient is any feed constituent or group of feed constituents of the same general chemical composition or a pure chemical compound that aids in the support of life. These consist of carbohydrates, protein, minerals, vitamins and water.

Feedstuff is synonymous with feed, food or fodder although it is broader, covering all materials included in the diet because of their nutritional properties. It includes natural feeds of animal origin, synthetic and other pure nutrients which are added in the natural feeds.

Feed is a mixture of feedstuff blended/processed in a form which is acceptable to animals. It is merely the carrier of nutrient and potential energy in a ration.

Supplement is a feed/feed mixture used with another feed to improve the nutritive balance of total ration and it is intended to be fed undiluted as a supplement to other feeds. It could be:

- Offered free choice with other parts of the rations separately available
- Further diluted and mixed to produce a complete feed.

A ration is an allowance of feed given to an animal over a specified period of time, e.g. daily ration or weekly ration. It should furnish the entire nutrient required in adequate amount.

Diet connotes a feed which is offered to an animal over a non-specified period of time. It is formulated for special purposes–experimentation, special physiological conditions (sick, production); a ration is part of a diet.

Dry matter is made up of inorganic and organic substances. The in-organic matter is composed of minerals or ash. The organic substances consist of combustible material, such as sugar, starch, fat, protein and fiber.

Ash is an inorganic constituent present in small quantities in all feeds and in all parts of the body. It is a non combustible material.

Nitrogen free extract is made up mostly of starches and sugars. It is used by the body for fuel which furnishes energy and heat.

Protein- energy ratio means the amount of protein in the feed or group of feeds as compared with the combined carbohydrates and fat. When we say a ration has a protein – energy ratio of 1 to 5, we mean that it contains one part of protein to every five parts of carbohydrates and fat.

3.2   Classification of Feed Ingredients

In discussing the many ingredients which may be useful in poultry diets/ rations, it seems logical to group them on the basis of the nutrients which they contain. The classification used here will be (1) carbohydrates, (2) protein, (3) fats, (4) mineral, (5) vitamin and (6) water.

3.2.1 Carbohydrates

Carbohydrates which are the major source of energy in poultry
diets include:

> The grains – maize, guinea corn, millet, wheat and broken rice. Cereal by-products – maize bran or offal, wheat bran or offal, rice bran or offal and guinea-corn offal.
>
> Starch roots and tubers – cassava flour, cassava chips and sweet potato. The dietary inclusion of 30–60% of these energy sources into the poultry diet is recommended with the upper limits mainly for young growing animals.

3.2.2 Protein

Commonly used, protein feed ingredients for poultry ration formulation and feeding includes the following:

- Vegetable/plant sources such as groundnut cake, soyabean cake, full-fat soybean, cotton seed cake and palm kernel cake.
- Animal protein sources such as fishmeal, meat and bone meal, blood meal.

3.2.3 Fats

Considerable quantities of fats are used in poultry feeding, primarily as potent source of energy. Fats normally contain two to three times as much metabolizable energy per unit of weight as grains. Major sources available are vegetable oil (palm oil, groundnut oil, soybean oil), hard fat, soft fat and hydrolyzed animal fat.

The usual practical limit for adding fats is 3 to 5 per cent of the diet, although with special technique pelleted diets may contain as high as 7 or 8 per cent added fat. Rations very high in fat tend to cake and do not flow readily.

3.2.4 Minerals

Sources of the major minerals for poultry rations include bone meal, limestone, oyster shell, di-calcium phosphate, de-fluorinated phosphate, common salt and trace mineral premixes.

3.2.5 Vitamins

The vitamins are commercially available in pure form or as vitamin concentrate at relatively low cost. They can be added to a poultry feed by means of a premix which supplies specified amounts of each vitamin. Certain ingredients available for poultry feeding are potent sources of vitamins. These include yeast, fat solubles, distillers' solubles, liver meal, alfalfa meal and milk by-products. All the fat soluble vitamins (A, D, E, and K) are supplied by fats and oils.

3.2.6 Water

Some water is available in the feed itself (metabolic water), but the bulk of it must be separately provided in drinking cans. Cool, clean water should be provided at all times. The water should be free from the excess salt which might have a laxative effect.

3.3   Anti Nutritional Factors

The nutrient potentials of some ingredients are limited by the presence of toxins, notable examples of which is guinea corn containing tannin, and cotton seed containing gossypol. Diets containing cotton seed cake therefore require supplementation with ferrous sulphate, apart from lysine, for balancing amino acids. Groundnut can develop Aspergillus flavus which produces aflatoxin that damages the liver. Soya beans contain trypsin inhibitor a growth depressant, meals produced from unprocessed beans should not be fed to poultry of the adverse effects.

3.4   Feeding Practices

3.4.1 Feed Presentation

The success of raising poultry depends very much on adequate feeding of the birds. Feed is offered to poultry at all times (*ad libitum*) or controlled (restricted).

3.4.1.1 The Unrestricted/*ad Libitum* Feeding Programme

Feed must be available to the birds at all times. This practice is commonly referred to as *ad libitum* feeding. This method of feeding allows the poultry to consume feed to appetite or want. Birds raised for meat (broilers) are preferably fed *ad libitum*.

Advantages

- More uniform body weight attainment at maturity.
- Feed management technique is less complicated as compared to feeding regimen in feed restriction programmes.
- Birds that feed themselves at will are less stressed up.

Disadvantages

- Birds overeat and increase feed cost during the rearing period.
- Meat type (broiler) breeders tend to overeat and grow excessively, thus compromising production efficiency and profitability (more small/peewee eggs prolapse etc).
- Overweight broiler breeders are prone to prolapse, reduced fertility, hatchability and reproductive failures.

3.4.1.2 The Restricted/Controlled Feeding Programme

Feed is supplied to the birds in limited quantity and/quality. The strains of birds must be grown on the controlled feeding programme to limit weight, particularly with broiler breeder strains. The female feed intake may be adjusted to delay egg at sexual maturity to maintain desired body weight and reduce prolapses. If the birds are overweight, some form of feed restriction may be imposed. It is advisable to start the restricted feeding programme from 6 weeks of age, although some breeders recommend earlier ages (2–3 weeks of age).

Advantages

- Reduction in the cost of feeding the birds during the growing period.
- Feed restriction results in later maturing birds that lay larger eggs at the initial period.
- The birds are less fat, thus protecting the birds from breeding problems due to excess fat.
- It leads to the production of more hatchable eggs during the laying year.

Disadvantages

- Management of the restricted feeding programme is more complicated than *ad libitum* feeding.
- Birds may be more uneven in body size mainly because of the differential feed intake of "boss" vs "timid" birds.
- It is more troublesome to feed the birds because they fight among themselves in a bid to get at the feed.
- Increase in cannibalism and mortality problems.

3.4.2 Forms of Feeds

The different kinds of chicken feeds are all available as commercially or home manufactured feeds. Commercial feeds in most cases will come in the form of a dry mixture called mash and sometimes pellets or crumbles. Whether commercial or home-mixed, feeds must match the different protein needs of chicks, grower, broiler and layers. It is the protein content which distinguishes what feed should be given to these different ages and types of chicken. Among the ways of feeding chickens are:

1. The all mash system: It is the use of a complete ground feed. It is well adapted to use with the mechanical feeding system.

a) **Wet Mash** – Chicken usually eat more wet mash than dry because they enjoy its consistency. However, wet mashes, particularly in hot weather, go bad very quickly, hence only an amount which will be consumed within two hours should be fed.

b) **Dry mash** – when it is well balanced and stored properly, dry mash usually is the best way of feeding confined chickens. It is commercially sold with these designations:

- Chick mash – contains 20 per cent protein
- Grower mash – contains 16 – 17 per cent protein
- Broiler mash – feed contain 20 – 23 per cent protein
- Layer mash – contains 15 – 17 per cent protein.

2. **Pellets or Crumbles:** Commercial mixtures in pellet or crumble forms are excellent but usually cost more than mash. Chickens may produce slightly better with the

pelleted/crumble forms. Pellet and crumble feeds reduce feed waste and the chickens may eat them a little better.

3.   **Whole Grain:** Feed is often used for whole grain, either by itself or mixed with other nutrients. Sometimes whole grain is scattered in the litter. The whole grain method of feeding is not recommended. When fed in with other ingredients, the grain is eaten first, resulting in improper diets; when scattered, much is contaminated or lost.

4.   The cafeteria system allows the birds to balance their own rations. Grain is fed in one feeder and a high (26%) protein supplement is fed in another feeder. Feed is kept in feeders at all times. Older birds may tend to eat too much grain and not enough protein supplements when this system is used.

3.5   Tips to Achieving a High Feed Efficiency

1.   Adequate feeding space should be provided at all times, ensuring that about 75% of the birds can feed at the same time.
2.   Feeders should be well designed with lips to prevent feed wastage.
3.   Feeders should be filled to not more than ½ full capacity.
4.   Feeders should be properly hung, ensuring that the level of feeders correspond to the back of the chicken and activate the feed in the feeders regularly with the hands.
5.   To avoid feed contamination and wastage, rat population should be constantly kept low.
6.   Attendants should minimize feed spillage during the process of serving feed to reduce wastage.
7.   Do not store feeds for too long or in damp places, otherwise they can become mouldy.

If there is any need to change from one type of feed to another it should be done gradually because chickens respond adversely to an abrupt switch over from one type of feed to another. This can be done spanning a period of about four days. The change can be effected by gradually increasing the quantity of the new feed to be changed to while there is corresponding decrease in the quantity of the feed currently in use.

4.0   CONCLUSION

This unit shows how you can raise poultry successfully based on feeding principles. It also discusses common terms used in poultry feeding, the roles of feed ingredients in poultry rations and the forms of feed offered to the birds. Tips to achieving high feed efficiency are equally addressed.

5.0   SUMMARY

You are expected to have learnt the following:

*   Principles of feeds and feeding in poultry production

*   Definitions of terms used in feeds and feeding
*   Feed ingredient classification based on nutrient supply
*   The different types of feeding programmes and
*   The different forms of feed presentation.

6.0   ASSIGNMENT

1.   Classify feed ingredients into various categories of nutrient supply.
2.   Define these concepts in poultry feeding.

(a)   Nutrient   (b)   Feeds   (c)   Supplement
(d)   Ration   (e)   Diet

3.   Briefly outline the disadvantages of poultry feeding programmes.

4.   List three common sources of protein for poultry rations.
5.   List three forms in which commercially manufactured chicken feeds may be purchased.
6.   What are the advantages of *ad libitum* feeding?

7.0   REFERENCES

Ogundipe, S. O. (1992). *Management of Laying Flock*. In Revamping Poultry Production Management and Feeding. Training Manual. Proceedings of NAPRI Poultry Workshop.

Oluyemi, J. A. and F. A. Roberts (2000). *Poultry Production in Warm Wet Climates* (2nd ed). Ibadan: Spectrum Books Limited. Pp. 147 – 168.

Rice, J. E. and Botsford, H. E. (1959). *Practical Poultry Management* (6th ed). New York & London: John Wiley and Sons, Inc. Pp. 118

UNIT 2   NUTRIENT REQUIREMENTS OF POULTRY

CONTENTS

1.0   Introduction
2.0   Objectives
3.0   Main Content
    3.1   Nutrient Requirements of Poultry
        3.1.1 Energy Requirements
        3.1.2 Protein Requirements
        3.1.3 Mineral Requirements
        3.1.4 Vitamin Requirements
        3.1.5 Water Requirements
    3.2   Nutrient Requirements and Factors Affecting Them
4.0   Conclusion
5.0   Summary
6.0   Assignment
7.0   References

1.0   INTRODUCTION

The requirement for any nutrient may be defined as the amount of that nutrient which must be supplied in the diet to meet the needs of the normal healthy animal, given an otherwise completely adequate diet in an environment compatible with good health. Such a level of nutrient must be capable of meeting the requirements for maintenance, optimum growth and reproductive potential of the animal.

Simply defined, nutrient requirement is the amount of a given nutrient required by the animal to maximize performance but not necessarily maximize profit. Maximum performance may however occur at different nutrient levels depending on the response criteria being considered, e.g. a specified rate of growth, or a stated level of production. The nutrient levels or requirements are expressed in the amount of nutrient per kilogramme of air dry feed (i.e. feed as fed) or in terms of percentages on as fed basis (air dry basis).It should be emphasized that the recommendations are merely guidelines and circumstances on individual farms may require adjustments.

2.0 OBJECTIVES

After studying this unit you should be able to:

- state clearly nutrient requirements of poultry
- list and state clearly the nutrient requirements of chickens.

- identify factors affecting nutrient requirements.

3.0   MAIN CONTENT

3.1   The Nutrient Requirements of Poultry

This topic will be discussed under the following five sub-headings:

1.   Energy requirements
2.   Protein requirements
3.   Mineral requirements
4.   Vitamin requirements
5.   Water requirements

3.1.1 Energy Requirements

The largest single dietary need of an animal is for a source of energy. Energy is required for all processes of life. Without energy birds cannot move, eat, digest, grow, maintain body temperature and, in the case of layers produce eggs. The requirements for energy cannot be stated as precisely as the requirements for protein, amino acids, minerals and vitamins. This is because good growth and egg production can be achieved with a wide range of energy levels. Most chickens have the ability to adjust feed intake in order to obtain the necessary energy required for optimum performance.

 Chicks aged day-old to 4–6 weeks are however not able to adjust feed intake to diet energy variations and thus tend to consume slightly more energy as the energy level of the diet increases. Not all energy eaten by the chicks is used. The energy that is used is called metabolizable energy (ME) and is measured in terms of kilocalories or kilojoules. Other energy is rejected in faeces. The energy levels recommended for broiler chickens (3000 kcal/kg diet) are lower than those (3200, 2900 and 2900 kcal/kg diet respectively) recommended or assumed for temperate zones of America. The reasons for these observations are obvious. At high temperatures, heat losses and basal metabolic rates are generally lower than those at lower temperatures. This means that at high temperatures, the energy is used more for reproductive and productive purpose and less on non-productive purposes. It is not therefore surprising that the energy requirements of poultry reared in the hotter tropical environment are lower.

3.1.2 Protein Requirements

The protein requirement is one of the most important criteria upon which any feed formula is based and if it is to be specified, the dietary energy level must be specified because it is essential to maintain the proper ratio of protein to energy in poultry diets. Protein needs for maintenance are relatively low, and therefore the requirement depends primarily on the amounts needed for productive purposes. To properly meet the protein requirements, the essential amino acids must be supplied in the proper amounts; and the total level of nitrogen in the diet must be high enough and in the proper form to permit synthesis of the non-essential amino acids.

Once the minimum amount of protein required supporting maximum growth rate or egg production is supplied, additional protein is oxidized for energy. The crude protein required in a layers diet has been reported to vary from 15 to 18 per cent which is lower than the requirement for pullet chicks (20%) and broilers (20-23%), since protein sources are expensive component of a ration, it is not economical to feed excess protein to animals. For this reason protein levels in diets for poultry are usually stated in precise terms to be closer to the minimum requirements than other nutrients. The recommended protein levels decrease as the chickens get older. Under normal circumstances, birds eat more as they grow older. Therefore the total protein consumed increases as the birds gets older and presumably increases in weight. However, the protein consumed per unit weight either reduces or remains constant.

The amino acid levels are expressed as percentages of the diets and decrease as the recommended protein level decreases.

3.1.3 Mineral Requirements of Poultry

Minerals are basic elements required for skeletal tissue development and maintenance. Special mention must be made of the recommended levels of calcium and phosphorus, particularly for "layers", because of the roles these two minerals play in egg formation. The levels of calcium and total phosphorus recommended for commercial layers (for table egg production) and breeders (for hatching chicks) are respectively 3.5% and 0.85%. The requirements for these minerals appear to be higher for warm climates than the cold climates. As a general rule, a level of 4-4.5% calcium and 1-1.1% total phosphorus should be provided at all times for birds reared in the tropics. In practice, 0.30-0.50% common salt or sodium chloride would take care of the requirements for sodium and chloride by all classes of poultry. All other macro – minerals are provided in ample amounts by the usual natural ingredients used in formulating poultry feeds. The micro–elements are often included in most commercial premixes. The amount of a micro–element is sometimes expressed in parts per million (ppm) or milligrams per kilogram of diet. In practice, about double the amount of premixes added to chicken diets should be used in turkey diets.

3.1.4 Vitamin Requirements

Vitamins are organic compounds required in extremely small quantities but essential for normal growth, health and productivity. Unlike protein, vitamins are usually supplied to poultry feeds in excess of their minimum requirements. However, if only minimum levels are provided, variations of expected feed consumption must be considered, and very high energy rations must be more liberally supplied with vitamins than low energy rations. Requirements are expressed in international units (I.U) which are the same as United States Pharmacopoeia units (U.S.P.). Most requirements for poultry are precisely known, particularly for those vitamins likely to be deficient in practical rations. Rations for young starting chicks and starting broilers are usually very liberally supplied with supplemental vitamins. Dietary vitamins premix inclusion is at the rate of 2.0-2.5 kg/tonne of feed. There are 13 vitamins listed as required by the chickens. The vitamins are classified as fat soluble vitamins (A, D, E and K) and water soluble vitamins (the B-complex vitamins and vitamins C).

3.1.5 Water Requirements

The quantities of water required by one hundred layers is about or over 24 litres per day or about one – quarter of a litre per bird per day. Normally, poultry consumes about 2 -3 parts of water for every part of feed on a weight basis (i.e. 2 to 3 kg water per kg consumed feed). Depending on the age, turkey should be provided with about two to five times the amount of water recommended for pullets. During hot weather, consumption of water may rise to about 4-5 times the intake of feed. This has been suggested as being responsible for inadequate feed intake in the tropics.

3.2   Nutrient Requirements and Factors Affecting Them

Certain factors affect the levels of nutrients required for the optimum performance of animals. Some of these factors will be discussed as follows:

1.   **Environmental Temperature:** This has a marked effect on energy requirement and hence the feed intake. Animals tend to eat less in warm than in cold environments. Research has shown that for every 5_oC change in pen temperature, there is about 20 kcal change in the ME intake of birds. Pen temperatures of 18 to 24_oC are within the normal comfort zone of poultry.

2.   **Energy Content of the Diet:** Poultry generally tend to eat to meet their energy requirements if fed *ad libitum* (i.e. if fed free choice). To put it another way, over a wide range of metabolizable energy (ME) concentration per unit weight of a balanced diet, and if fed *ad libitum*, most poultry will likely adjust feed intake in order to provide fixed ME consumption. Thus ME consumption is more likely to be constant than total feed intake. Chickens fed low energy diets will eat more feed than those fed high energy diets. Therefore, the amount of required nutrients in poultry rations must be adjusted in relation to the energy level in the ration in order to ensure that the birds consume the right amount of needed nutrient.

3.   **Productive State of the Animal:** The broiler chicken and turkey poult have high requirements for amino acids to meet the needs for rapid growth; the mature cockerel has a very low requirement than the laying hen, even though body size is actually greater and feed consumption is similar; high egg producing hens would require more nutrients than low egg producing hens.

3.   **Sex:** Cockerels need more energy than pullets and chickens.

4.   **Age:** Nutrient requirements change with the age of the animal.

5.   **Size of the Animal:** Large animals (broiler finisher, matured turkey) need more feed and hence more nutrients than spent layers.

6.   **Effects of Diseases (Ill-Health and Infection):** Diseases and the presence of internal parasites, coccidia, bacteria or external parasites may affect feed intake and the requirements for certain nutrients. Infection reduces feed intake. Poultry recovering from illness need more energy and nutrients than healthy birds.

7.   **Balance between Nutrients**: This may affect the metabolic utilization of individual nutrients and hence their requirements, e.g. dietary protein level versus individual amino acids, vitamin D, calcium and phosphorus interrelationship.

8.   **The Presence of Toxic Factors in Feeding-Stuffs:** Linamarin in cassava products increases the need for methionine, gossypol in cotton seed; trypsin inhibitor in soyabeans; progoitrin in canola seed; toxins from field fungi; aflatoxin in groundnut cake.

9.   **System of Management:** This may affect recommended nutrient levels of poultry in terms of the floor or cage rearing; intensive or extensive system of management.

4.0 CONCLUSION

Nutrient requirements are known more precisely for poultry. This has come about because of the economic importance of the poultry industry. Proper poultry rations can be devised only by application of the nutritional information known about the class of poultry to be fed. The application of this information to poultry feeding requires the knowledge of nutrients, the feedstuffs to supply these nutrients, and the amount of nutrient needed for the particular productive purpose.

5.0 SUMMARY

In this unit we have been able to define nutrient requirement and examined the importance of nutrients in promoting body metabolism and productivity. We also examined factors affecting the level of nutrient requirements for optimum performance of poultry.

6.0 ASSIGNMENT

1.   Define nutrient requirement.

2. List the nutrients commonly required in a chicken ration.
3. What factors affect the nutrient requirement of poultry?

7.0 REFERENCES

Gillespie, J. R. (1992). *Modern Livestock and Poultry Production* (4th ed.) Delmar Publishing Inc., pp 611.

UNIT 3   BREEDS AND BREEDINGS

CONTENTS

1.0   Introduction
2.0   Objectives
3.0   Main Content
    3.1   Definition of Breed
    3.2   Yardsticks for Breed Recognition
    3.3   Breeds of Domestic Poultry
    3.4   Principles of Breeding
    3.5   Advantages of Breeding
    3.6   Traits of Economic Importance
    3.7   Management of Breeding Stock
4.0   Conclusion
5.0   Summary
6.0   Assignment
7.0   References

1.0   INTRODUCTION

Breeds of poultry today are better than they were one hundred years ago. They have improved egg numbers, egg weight, fertility, hatchability growth rate, body conformation, meat yield, egg and meat quality and variability that maximize the efficiency of production and increase profitability. Much of this progress in poultry efficiency is the result of the use of genetics. Good breeding programmes are based on an application of the principles of genetics. Poultry breeders use this to select birds for breeding that will produce offspring with desirable characteristics.

2.0   OBJECTIVES

After studying this unit, you should be able to:

- define a breed
- explain how genetics relates to improvement in poultry production

- identify and describe the physical appearance of the different breeds of poultry
- state briefly the principles of breeding.

3.0 MAIN CONTENT

3.1 Definition of Breed

A breed is a group of related individual (poultry) that possesses the same ancestry and breeds true for a number of characteristics that identify the breed. Breed recognition is conferred by a recognized breeders' association that registers the breed.

3.2 Yardsticks for Breed Recognition

1. Shape is generally accepted as the main yardstick in breed recognition, the black leghorn and the ancona differ not in shape but in a single gene which causes mottling in the latter.
2. Varietal differences exist in plumage colour and comb type within breeds.
3. Head and leg characteristics of mendelian in heritance.
4. Shell colour is a breed characteristic and appears to be due to the interaction of several genes.
5. Body weight – light and heavy breeds.
6. Skin colour – yellow and white.
7. Origin – breeds can be characterized to a great extent through their places of origin.

3.3 Breeds of Domestic Poultry

1. Chicken Breeds

a) White Leghorn

- The best layer of white eggs
- Plumage white uniformly
- Well-developed wattle and crest (comb)
- The crest is erect in males and droopy in hens
- The leghorn hen rarely exceeds 2.5kg and the cocks 2.5-3.5kg.
- Flesh is meagre
- Beak and shank white – creamy colour

b) White Wyandotte

- Plumage colour is white
- Beak and shank are yellowish
- Crest is triple
- Flesh is yellowish
- Lay large brown eggs
- It is a hardy breed
- It's a heavy breed (3-4kg)

c) Rhode Island Red

- It has brilliant plumage that is dark red
- With mahogany brown flecks on the collar
- The wings, tail and sickle feathers are very dark, black or greenish
- Feet are yellowish
- Flesh is yellowish
- Hens weights about 3kg and males 4.5k
- It is a hardy breed
- Lays tinted/brown eggs.
- Beak black to brown

d) Barred Plymouth Rock

- It has streaks of grey and white plumage giving a bluish striped appearance
- It has triple crest
- It has yellow feet
- It weighs between 3.0kg female – 3.9kg cocks
- It lays brown/tinted eggs
- Yellowish flesh
- Well adaptable to tropical environment
- Beak is greyish – white
- Free rangers/vigorous foragers

e) New Hampshire

- It has mahogany red plumage which is brighter in cock and darker in the hens
- Feet are light yellowish.
- Flesh is white 10 less yellowish than R.I.R.
- It lays brown eggs

- The males weight about 3kg and 4kg in cocks
- It is a mixed breed

f)   Light Sussex

- It is a pure white breed with napped feathers streaked with black
- The tail is black
- Feet are grey
- Beak is greyish – cream
- Lays tinted eggs
- Males weight about 4kg and females about 3kg
- Flesh white to creamy
- It is a calm breed

g)   Harco (R I R. x. Barred Plymouth Rock)

- Male entirely black with mahogany collar while female grey and white

2.   Breeds of Turkey

a)   The Broad Breasted Bronze

- Black plumage and dark–coloured pin feathers
- Females have white tips on the black breast feathers.
- The beard is black in males
- Females normally do not have beards
- Shanks and feet are pinkish
- The beak is light at the tip and dark at the base
- It is the largest of the turkey varieties, stags – 22kg females – 18 kg.
- Fewer eggs with low fertility and hatchability
- Artificial insemination is generally used – heavy males are not good breeders.

b)   The Broad Breasted Large White

- Developed from crosses of the broad breasted bronze and the white Holland.
- Plumage colour is white
- Males have a black beard
- Some females have very small beards

- The shanks, feet and the beak are white to pinkish white
- Has a good body conformation

c)   Norfolk Black

- Good meat conformation
- Medium sized birds, stags 7-8kg, hens 4-5kg,
- Plumage is black
- Black quill in skin, low carcass value
- Ninety eggs/year

3.   Breeds of Ducks

The wild mallard (*Anas boschas*) is generally regarded as the ancestor of all domestic breeds of ducks (*Anas platyrhynchos*). The best breeds of ducks for meat production are the white pekin, Aylesbury and muscovy. Other meat producing breeds include the rouen, cayuga, Swedish welsh harleguins and call. The best egg – laying breeds are the khaki campbells and Indian runners.

a)   The White Pekin

- Generally used for commercial meat production
- Originated from China and brought to U. S.
- Reaches market weight at 8 weeks (3.2kg)
- They have white feathers
- Orange – yellow bills
- Reddish – yellow shanks and feet and yellow skin
- Eggs are tinted white
- Poor setters (will not sit on a nest of eggs) seldom raise a brood
- The breed nervous

b)   The Aylesbury

- Originated from England
- The same size at the white pekin (3-3.5kg)
- Have white feathers, skin–flesh, coloured bills
- Light – orange legs and feet
- Eggs are tinted white
- Do not set well.
- Seldom raise a brood

c)   **Khaki Campbell**

- Originated in England

- Excellent egg producers (365 eggs/ duck / year)
- The drake is khaki coloured with a brownish-bronze lower back, tail, convert, head and neck.
- The bill is green
- Legs and toes are dark orange
- The females are khaki coloured with seal brown heads and necks.
- The female's bill is greenish – black and the legs and toes are brown.
- At 8 weeks of age female (1.8kg) male (2.00kg)

d)   **The Muscovy**
- Generic name; *Cairina moschata*
- Originated in South America
- The quite muscovy is the best meat duck of the muscovy varieties
- White plumage and skin
- The adult drake (4.5kg) and adult duck (3.2kg)
- They are good setters and hatches well.

4.   **Breeds of Geese**

a)   **Embden**

- White breed
- Originated from Germany
- It is the largest of the utility birds
- Produces a fine carcass for the table
- Adult gander weighs about 1.8kg
- The adult goose weighs about 9.1kg
- Produces fewer eggs (40 eggs/ season)
- Have orange bills
- Pale–reddish shanks and foes

b)   **The Toulouse**

- Originated from France
- It is a dark grey with a white abdomen
- It has large fold of skin (dewlap) that hangs down from the throat of the upper and of the neck

- Has a pale – orange bill
- Deep reddish – orange shanks and toes
- Adult gander – 11.0kg
- Adult goose – 8kg
- Lay about – 40 eggs / season

c)   The Chinese

- Originated from China from wild goose
- They are graceful and swan – like in appearance and are either white or brown.
- Excellent foragers
- Shanks are pinkish reddish bill is brown
- Lay more eggs than any other breed (100 eggs / season)
- Adult gander (5.4kg)
- Adult goose (4.5kg)

d)   The African

- Is grey with a brown shade
- It has a knob on its beak and has a dewlap
- The knob and bill are black
- The head is light brown
- Adult gander weighs 9.1kg
- Adult goose weighs 8.2kg

5.   The Guinea Fowl

Numida Meleagris

- Basically wild birds

3.4 Principles of Breeding

The fundamental principles of scientific breeding are:

1. Breeding should be purposeful: the breeder should have a clear focus about the traits to which the animals are to be bred e.g. egg production or weight of broiler.

2. Parents to be used for breeding purposes must be as nearly purebred as possible in order to be able to breed true.

3. Selection must be carried out continually and carefully, both in regard to mating and culling of inferior progeny. Selected animals

to become parents in the next generation and the number of progeny they will be allowed to contribute.

4. Breeding should be done from parents that conform as closely as possible to the required standard. This is because the objective of selection for performance or qualitative trait is to increase the frequency of the combinations of genes that permit the animal that is most suitable for the given environment.

5. Environmental conditions play an important part in breeding. Conditions that are as near the ideal as possible should be created in respect of housing, feeding, health and general care.

3.5 Advantages of Breeding

Chicken provides one of the best models to test theory and practical of the principles of breeding. Some of the advantages are:

1. Breeding practices aim at genetic improvement of the poultry through successive generation.
2. Poultry breeding improves those qualities that have a definite market value, such as increased egg product and egg weight etc.
3. Breeding concentrates on the animal: what it really is, what it received from its progenitors and what it will pass to is offspring.
4. It shortens generation intervals.
5. It involves some modifications of the animals' external environment (nutrition, health and husbandry systems).

3.6 Traits of Economic Importance

- Egg production (layers)
- Egg weight (layers)
- Body size and conformation (broilers)
- Feed efficiency (Broilers and Layer)
- Fertility/ hatchability (broilers layers).

3.7 Management of Breeding Stock

The success of a broiler flock management starts from the selection of the breed, strain or variety of birds to rear. The prevailing market needs must be considered in selection and attempts must be made to meet these needs using the birds selected as economically as possible. The demand for brown versus white eggs, efficiency of feed utilization, rate of egg production and the livability of the type of birds, are some of the parameters to be considered. The breeders flock must be kept healthy and provided with a breeder diet adequate to supply the fertile egg with all the nutrients necessary, not only for embryonic development, but also to maintain the offspring in a healthy condition until it consumes adequate feed.

Breeder hens that are in poor health frequently either fail to supply the embryo with some vital nutritional factors or perhaps pass some toxic material to the egg; thus the hatch is poor or the chicks are of poor quality and must be culled. Breeder flock must be vaccinated during the growing period to prevent disease occurrence and onward egg transmission during the laying period.

In-breeding must be avoided by using studs or cocks should be less than ten months and the hens should normally be in their second year of lay in order to increase fertility and hatchability.

4.0 CONCLUSION

We have defined breed and the yardsticks for breed recognition. The unit also revealed to us the advantages of breeding, the general characteristics of breeds of poultry and traits of economic importance.

5.0 SUMMARY

The main points in this unit are:

- What the definition of breed is
- Yardsticks for breed recognition
- General characteristics of poultry breeds
- Fundamental principles of scientific breeding and traits of economic importance.

6.0 ASSIGNMENT

1. Outline five characteristics each of the breeds of domesticated geese.
2. What are the principles of breeding?
3. List the advantages of breeding.
4. What are the traits of the economic importance in a poultry breeding programme?

7.0 REFERENCES/FURTHER READINGS

Abubakar, B.Y and Oni, O.O.(2002). *Practical Poultry Breeding and Selection Methods*. In Training Manual: Poultry Production in Nigeria, NAPRI Shuka, Nigeria. Pp 1-9.

Oluyemi, J.A. and Roberts, F. A. (2000). Poultry *Production in Warm Wet Climates*. Ibadan: Spectrum Books Ltd Pp 18-34.

MODULE 3 RAISING OF POULTRY TO OBTAIN POULTRY PRODUCTS

Unit 1   Brooding of Chicks
Unit 2   Rearing of Chicks
Unit 3   Production of Egg and Broilers
Unit 4   Processing and Marketing of Poultry and Poultry Products

UNIT 1   BROODING OF CHICKS

CONTENTS

1.0   Introduction
2.0   Objectives
3.0   Main Content
        3.1   Brooding
                3.1.1 Brooding Methods
                3.1.2 The Brooder
                        3.1.2.1 The Surround or Guard Brooder
                        3.1.2.2 The Battery Brooder
                        3.1.2.3 The Tier Brooder
                3.1.3 Preparation for the Arrival of Chicks
                3.1.4 Handling of Chicks on Arrival
                3.1.5 Management of Chicks in the Brooder
4.0   Conclusion
5.0   Summary
6.0   Tutor-Marked Assignment
7.0   References/Further Readings

1.0   INTRODUCTION

Poultry keeping is an age-long tradition of Nigerian farmers. Most farming families in rural areas and an average percentage of households in towns and cities across the country keep flocks of chickens, turkeys, guinea fowls, ducks and a few other poultry species as a source of extra income, for meeting some social demands or as sacrificial animals. However, in the past four decades, the poultry industry in Nigeria has witnessed a significant transformation from traditional poultry rearing, using local chickens to the application of modern production techniques on the exotic strains of chicken which are more productive. This has resulted in the emergence of a number of commercial farms with a view to making the poultry industry a significant contributor to the animal protein pool of the nation. In spite of the remarkable growth of the poultry industry the production efficiency on most farms is very low giving, cause for concern on how to make the industry operate optimally. A critical factor identified for the dismal performance of the industry hammers on faulty production and management strategies. This unit therefore, focuses on the vital information the poultry farmer needs to have at his fingertips to enable him raise chicks successfully.

2.0   OBJECTIVES

By the end of the unit, you are expected to be able to:

- explain how to brood chicks
- identify necessary equipment and facilities for successful brooding
- explain and demonstrate how to prepare for the arrival of chicks
- distinguish between routine and periodic management practices.

3.0   MAIN CONTENT

3.1   Brooding

Brooding is the process of caring for young chicks from day-old to six weeks of age. It entails essentially, the provision of factors like heat, light, humidity, ventilation, feed, water and disease control measures for the survival and rapid growth of chicks. It is the efficient combination of these factors that determines the level of physical and physiological development and the mortality of the chicks. A brooder or a brooding unit is designed to house chicks from day-old until they no longer need supplementary heat between 0-8 weeks.

3.1.1 Brooding Methods

There are two general systems of brooding:

1. **The Natural Method:** This is the care of chicks by a mother hen. The local fowls are suitable for this method. Depending on her size, a hen can brood 12-20 chickens. This includes the chicks she hatches and the ones fostered on her when day-old chicks are placed with her. However before fostering, she should be examined for good health and mothering ability. This method is used where only few chickens are raised each year and not suitable for a commercial scale operation.

2. **The Artificial Method:** This involves the use of special appliances which provide conditions similar to those of the broody hen such as adequate warmth, protection from harsh external factors of weather (wind, rain, temperature) and predators. It also allows good feeding, watering and disease control. Artificial brooding is the best method for the commercial producer. Artificial brooding has some advantages over the natural method namely:

a) Chicks may be reared at any time of the year.
b) Thousands of chicks may be brooded at once depending on the capacity of the farmer.
c) Sanitary conditions may be controlled.
d) Temperature may be regulated and
e) Feeding may be controlled to meet the production objective.

3.1.2 The Brooder

A brooder consists of a source of heat and the area under the brooder where young chicks are raised. It is built and placed inside a chicken house and the area is enlarged till the chicks reach about 21 days when the brooder is dismantled. For heating brooders, use of coal, kerosene, gas, electricity is employed depending on the availability of these materials and the capacity of the farmer.

There are many types and sizes of brooder units in the market. The equipment is rated by the manufacturer according to the number of chicks that it can accommodate. The essentials of a good brooder are:

- A dependable mechanism for controlling temperature.
- Regular supply of fresh air, dryness
- Adequate light, space.
- Easy disinfection.
- Protection against chick enemies, safety from fire and
- Economy in construction.

The most popular type of brooder is probably the floor brooder with the hover providing the heat. This is characterized by a pyramidal or conical canopy of aluminum or galvanized iron mounted on metal legs. The canopy reflects heat to the back of the chick and should be kept clean on the under surface. All brooder boxes should be constructed with holes at the top (apex of the brooder) to provide for the escape of fumes especially when kerosene lamps are used. Directly below the apex of the brooder or close to it is the heating element or the source of heat.

3.1.2.1   The Surround or Guard Brooder

In floor-brooding, chicks should be restricted to within a short distance of the hover until they are fairly feathered and can locate the source of heat. They are restricted by a 40cm high surround, usually made of hardboard. Any shape is suitable, provided it is free from corners in which chicks can huddle. This brooder is recommended especially for very large projects but can be adapted for small number. The chicks will be managed in this enclosed area for 10-14 days and, as they grow older, the area can be extended to fill the entire chicken house.

Note that a brooding house should be able to conserve heat to keep the house warm. A brooding house should also be located not less than 45.5m away from other poultry houses in which older birds are stocked. This helps to curtail the risk of disease transference from old to young stock.

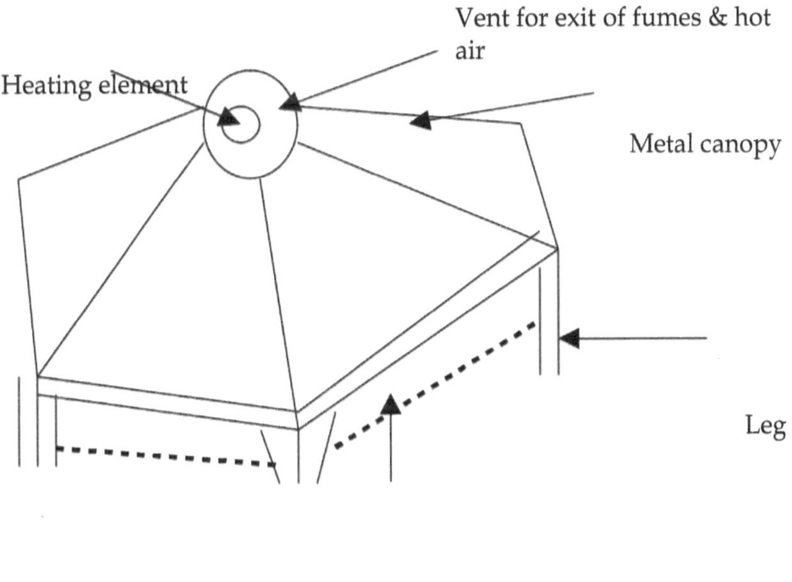

(a)   A metallic canopy floor brooder

(b)   Wooden canopy floor
        brooder (Refer to Module 1
        Unit 1).

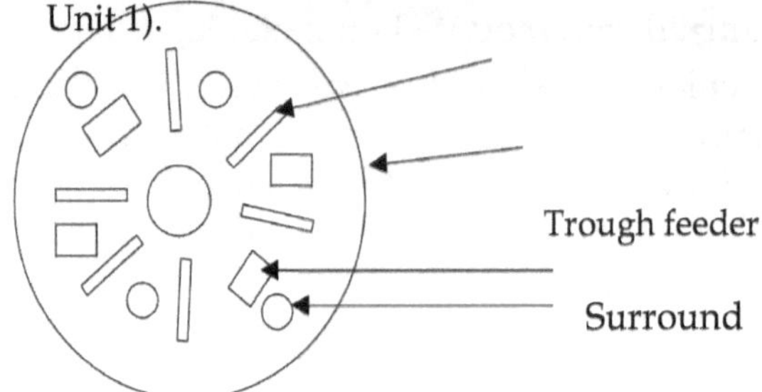

Flat feeder
Waterer

(c)   The Typical Brooder unit layout (floor layout)

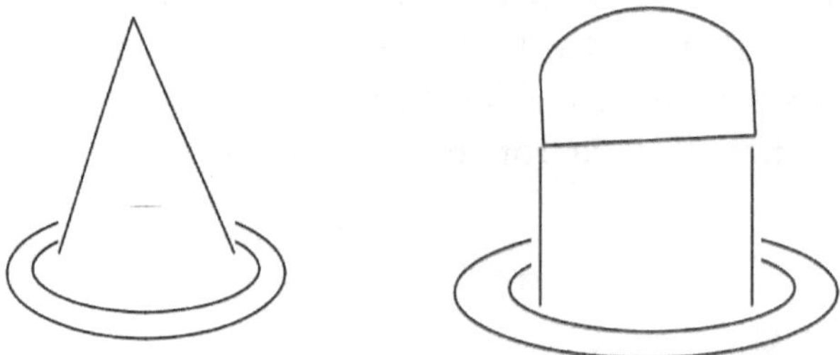

3.1.2.2   The Battery Brooder

This is in the form of a series of drawers (usually four) maintained at different temperatures. The brooder is heated by electricity or hot water provides heat uniformly in each compartment.

The advantages of the battery brooder are:

- Its convenience
- Chicks are free from contact with litter
- Chicks can be closely observed

Its disadvantages are:

- Chicks become overcrowded leading to cannibalism
- Its only suitable for started chicks.

- It does not provide access of chicks to cooler zones hence they become enervated and loosely feathered

3.1.2.3 The Tier Brooder

The problem of no access to cooler zones in the battery brooder is eliminated in the tier brooder as only a part of the brooder is heated. Like the battery brooder, it must be properly housed to allow adequate ventilation.

3.1.3 Preparation for the Arrival of Chicks

It is critical for the poultry farmer to take all necessary steps before he takes delivery of the day-old chicks. This will lessen stress on the chicks and increase their survival rate during brooding periods. It is advisable to start the preparations for brooding chicks about three weeks before their arrival. The following activities should be carried out:

1. Remove old litter from the house if already in use, remove cobwebs and dust on the wood frames, sweep the house and then thoroughly wash and disinfect the house using a suitable disinfectant like izal, dettol etc.
2. Repair the house if necessary- mend leaking roofs, plaster cracks on the wall and crevices on the floor, repair doors.
3. Feeders and drinkers should be thoroughly washed and disinfected.
4. The house should then be sealed up and fumigated if possible especially in buildings which are not open-sided.
5. If tier brooders, battery brooders or any other type of brooder is to be used, they should be brushed clean and then washed very clean of droppings.
6. The needed equipment should be purchased and tested to be functional.
7. The house should be left empty for a period of not less two weeks to destroy any surviving disease organizations through starvation.
8. Two days to the arrival of the chicks, the house should be swept and the equipment cleaned.
9. Spread litter material up to a depth of 5cm on the floor and test run again the heating system for its efficacy in heating up the brooder.
10. If a half open-sided house will be used, the open sides should be covered with plastic sheets, mats, empty feed bags or any other suitable material.
11. A few hours before the arrival of chicks, put on the heater, fill the

drinkers with clean cool water, put feed in the trough not more than a depth of one half and also sprinkle some on flat feeders which are adequate for the first week.

3.1.4 Handling of Chicks on Arrival

The following steps are important:

1.   The chicks should be unboxed and inspected individually for defects and apparently healthy ones should be put under the brooder hover. The deformed ones should be killed while the weak chicks are aided to drink water.
2.   After setting them up, they should be observed for some minutes to be sure that they are in a state of comfort.
3.   If the chicks spread evenly under the hover, they are considered comfortable. If they huddle in the centre close to the heater, they are cold and if they are far from the heater, then the brooder is too hot. Thus, the heater should be regulated to produce the right temperature.

3.1.5 Management of Chicks in the Brooder

The following steps are important:

1.   Adjust the temperature to meet the requirements of chicks.
2.   Discourage litter eating by the chicks by sprinkling mash over a flat tray on arrival and ensuring that there is feed always in the food trough.
3.   In the first week, inspect your flock as often as you can but without disturbing them. Early mornings and evenings are regular inspection times and may be at other times.
4.   Remove dead birds and bury them. Also isolate weak ones.
5.   Maintain a flow of fresh air.
6.   Remove mouldy or contaminated feed and add a fresh supply. Wet litter should likewise be treated.
7.   Wash the drinkers and clean the feeders daily and thereafter refill them with clean water and fresh feed respectively.
8.   Report abnormal signs observed to your veterinary officer promptly.
9.   Follow a regular vaccination programme. The schedule presented in Table 3.1is suitable for the Nigeria experience.
10. Avoid overcrowding as this will retard growth and mortality.
11. Keep records of everyday activities using forms designed for each activity.

12. Just before the chicks are moved to the grower house or if there is an evidence of worm infestation, ensure the chicks are dewormed.

Table 3.1: A Recommended Vaccination Programme

Age	Vaccine
1 day old	1st dose of Newcastle disease vaccine
	A dose of Marek's disease vaccine
2 weeks	1st dose of Gumboro disease vaccine
3-5 weeks	2nd dose of Gumboro disease vaccine (to be given 3 weeks after the 1st dose)
6-8 weeks	A dose of fowl pox vaccine
	2nd dose of New Castle disease vaccine
16-18 weeks	3rd dose of New Castle disease vaccine
18 weeks	3rd dose of Gumboro disease vaccine (Breeders only)

4.0 CONCLUSION

In this unit, you have been exposed to the importance of brooding and the technicalities therein for successful poultry raising.

5.0 SUMMARY

This unit teaches the following:

- Brooding as an art of caring for young chicks from day old to six weeks of age
- The elements required for a successful brooding
- Brooding methods and types of brooders
- How to prepare to receive and handle new chicks on the farm
- Management of chicks in the brooder.

6.0 ASSIGNMENT

1. Describe what you understand by brooding.
2. Differentiate between natural and artificial methods of brooding.
3. a. What is the equipment for brooding called? b. Itemize the essentials of this equipment.

4. Which of the types of brooder will you recommend for use in Nigeria and why?

5.   How would you get ready to receive a fresh batch of day-old chicks on your farm?
6.   How would you manage newly received chicks on your farm at the brooding phase?
7.   How would you handle newly hatched chicks on arrival on the farm?
8.   What are the advantages of the battery brooder?
9.   How would you handle newly hatched chicks on arrival on the farm?
10.   What are the advantages of the battery brooder?

7.0   REFERENCES/FURTHER READINGS

AERLS (1987). "Brooding and Rearing of Chicks on Deep Litter Floor." *Extension Bulletin* No. 33. Poultry Bulletin Services No. 2. AERLS, ABU Zaria Nigeria.

Smith, A. J. (1990). *The Tropical Agriculturist*. London & Basingstoke: Macmillan Education Ltd.

UNIT 2   REARING OF CHICKS

CONTENTS

1.0   Introduction
2.0   Objectives
3.0   Main Content
    3.1   Rearing
    3.2   Facilities and Equipment Required for Rearing
        3.2.1 Housing
        3.2.2 Feeding and Watering Troughs
        3.2.3 Miscellaneous Equipment
    3.3   Important Considerations in Rearing
4.0   Conclusion
5.0   Summary
6.0   Assignment
7.0   References

1.0   INTRODUCTION

The subject of discussion is still focused on raising of poultry chicks successfully in order to guarantee sustainable production and income. The emphasis in this unit is rearing of chicks.

2.0   OBJECTIVES

At the end of this unit, you should be able to:

- explain the importance of rearing to the overall concept of chicken production
- list and identify the essential equipment for rearing of chicks
- discuss the facilities needed for rearing.

3.0   MAIN CONTENT

3.1   Rearing

Rearing is the care of chicks from about seven weeks of age to the point they begin to drop eggs, i.e. point of lay. It can also be described as the care of growers. Rearing is critical to the overall success of the poultry industry because it ensures that the development of the birds at this stage of growth is satisfactory.

3.2   Facilities and Equipment Required for Rearing

Most of the facilities and equipment required to rear chicks are derived from those needed in brooding.

3.2.1 Housing

Houses for brooding can be constructed to serve this purpose and are so designated. They can also be designed to fit the rearing of chicks. When constructing a house, the following should be noted:

1.   **Foundation**: A strong foundation is required. Depending on the nature of the soil, digging should be done to a depth of between 0-5-7m or more. After digging a basement of a layer of concrete should be poured into a depth of 4cm. To control the effect of termites, an anti-termite chemical can be poured on top of this basement.

2.   **Floor**: Floor space allowances adequate for broilers and pullets are shown in Table 3.2.

Table 3.2:   Floor Space Requirements per Bird for Chickens of Different ages (m$_2$)

Age of Bird	Broiler		Pullet
(wks)		Floor	Cage (cm^2)
0-6	0.046	0.046	277
6-10	0.074	0.074	310
10-15		0.093	355
15-20		0.140	484
20-72		0.230	643

3.   **Walls**: Walls may be built up with cement or mud blocks. If it's to be open-sided, provision should be made for the erection of pillars at 1.3 to 1.6m apart. The solid portion of the wall should be one-third to half of the total height of the wall. Young chicks require warm environment up to about 6 to 8 weeks of age. Thereafter, the height of the wall need not be higher than 0.8m. Many small size and semi-commercial poultry farmers brood and rear the birds in the same house. It should be noted that the same open-sided house suitable for adult birds may be adapted for brooding chicks by covering the open sides with plastic sheets to conserve heat for the young birds during these first few weeks of life. If separate brooder house is available, then

the solid portion of the wall of the house for growers (8-20 weeks) and for layers (21 weeks and above) should not be more than 0.8m. If battery cages are to be used for growers or layers, the solid wall should not be higher than 0.8m. The height of the walls for the broiler house may be about 0.5 of the total height to the eaves.

4.   **Roof:** Roofing materials such as zinc and aluminum roofing sheets are good for poultry houses. Thatched roofing is not encouraged because of problems like fire and cleaning etc. A roof overhang of about 0.91m is required to prevent rain from entering the house through the open sides of the wall. A higher roof tends to make the house cooler if a ceiling is not provided.

5.   **Doors**: Doors should not be less than 0.9m to facilitate easy movement of staff, equipment, birds, and manure. A footbath of disinfectant is essential at the foot of each door.

6.   **Store**: Provision should be made for a space in the house to keep equipment, feed and other items for use in the house.

3.2.2 Feeding and Watering Troughs

These are used to feed and water growers. They are larger than the ones used in brooding. They provide more space per bird. Feeders may be longitudinal or conical in shape while a linear feeding space of 2.5m and depth of about 7.5cm is adequate for about 100 chicks from 0-6 weeks, the feeding space should be doubled for broiler chicks from 4-10 weeks and pullet chicks from 6-14 weeks. Also, for this age and beyond, the feeder should be about 15cm deep. This means that 100 chicks would need one 1.25m long feeder up to 4-6 weeks of age and two wider and deeper feeders for 100 birds up to 10 or 14 weeks of age. Beyond 14 weeks, 3 of such large feeders will be required for 100 pullets or layers.

Feeders should be constructed with lips to minimize feed wastage and be fitted with rollers at the open end to prevent birds from jumping in and contaminating the feed with their feaces. Most feeders are metallic or wooden troughs. However there are also tubes or hanging feeders (fig. 2).

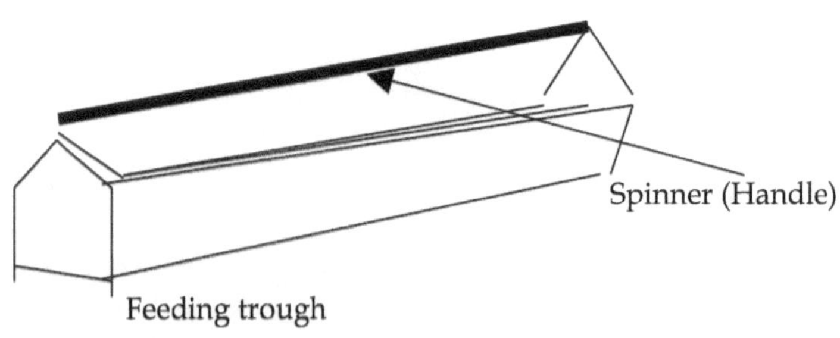

a)   A typical trough feeder

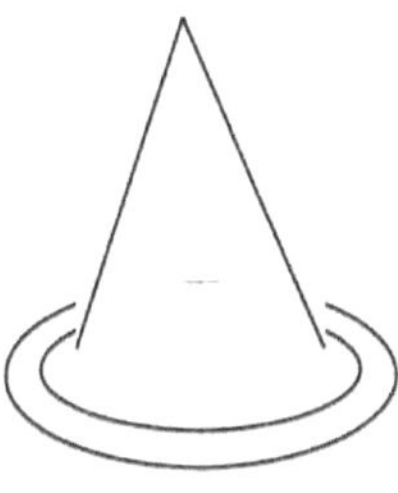

Conical drinkers feeder   A typical tube feeder

The commonest form of drinker available in Nigeria is the water fountain which may be made of galvanized iron, aluminum or plastic. The plastic if not handled with great care is not durable. It easily breaks. The iron type becomes rusty. The aluminum type is rust-resistant but expensive. They come in different sizes of between 2 to 6 or even 8 litres and are usually conical or cylindrical. While two chick size plastic drinkers of 2 litres capacity per 100 chicks are adequate between 1-4 weeks of age, thereafter bigger waterers should be used like two waterers of 10-15 litre capacity for 100 birds up to 20 weeks. Three of such waterers per 100 birds should be used thereafter. An ideal waterer is as shown in Module 1 unit 1(Refer to it).

In general, feeders and waterers are often constructed in two standard sizes. One for chicks and the other for older chickens. In addition, they are designed to minimize feed wastage and water spillage and to prevent the chicks from jumping into the feed or water and contaminating it.

3.2.3 Miscellaneous Equipment

In addition to the list above, the poultry farmer would require items like buckets, brooms, shovels, wheelbarrow, water storage tanks, weighing scale, office space and equipment.

3.3   Important Considerations in Rearing

1.   The growers need more ventilation than the chicks. Maximum ventilation will be guaranteed partly by using poultry houses with low sided walls (0.3m or less), a forced ventilation rate of $0.003m^3/s$ is

recommended to reduce ambient temperature and purify the atmosphere. Ventilation helps to provide the birds with fresh air and to carry off moisture.

2.   The growers require lower environmental temperatures than chicks. They require a moderate temperature but need a warmer temperature at night when they are inactive than during the day. A relative humidity of 50-80% is adequate for growers.

3.   Even though chicks are photo-sensitive, from as early as three weeks old, the effect of light is negligible until the fowl is 7 weeks old. When birds mature earlier than normal i.e. precocious maturity, due to inappropriate light pattern, it causes a depressed rate of lay and also reduced egg size because of low point-of-lay body weight. Growers between 4-20 weeks do not require extra light. The control of sexual maturity of the fowl depends largely on the pattern of the photo-period. The rule is that there must be a decrease in photo-period as the chick grows older.

4.   The growers are fed on a type of diet called growers mash. It is specially formulated to meet the energy, protein (amino acids), mineral and vitamin requirements of growers to achieve maximum growth and production potential. The feed for growers can be compounded by the farmer if he has the expertise or and bought from the sales outlets of commercial feed millers just like the feeds for other chickens at different stages of growth. Feed is the most important single factor in the production of poultry meat and eggs. It is therefore, important to know the feed consumption of your birds so that the right quantity can be purchased in advance in the course of rearing. However feeds should not be for over four weeks as they tend to become mouldy, stale and rancid if stored for too long. Table 3.3: gives the feed type, type of bird and estimated feed consumption (per 2 weeks) for broilers and pullets in a tropical environment.

Table 3.3: Feed Types and Consumption of Chicken

Age (wks)	Broiler			Pullet		
	Feed type	Feed Intake kg/bird	Bird	Feed type	Feed intake kg/bird	Bird
1	Broiler starter		Boiler chick	Chick mash		Chick
2	"	0.3	"	"	0.20	"
3	"		"	"		"
4	"	0.75	"	"	0.40	"
5	"		"	"		"

6	Broiler finisher	1.25	Broiler chicken	"	0.65	"
7	"		"	"		"
8	"	1.60	"	"	0.85	"
9	"		"	Grower mash		Pullets
10	"	1.90	"	"	0.90	"
11				"		"
12				"	1.00	"
13				"		"
14				"	1.10	"
15				"		"
16				"	1.15	"
17				"		"
18				"	1.15	"
19				"		"
20				"	1.30	"

5. The management system normally used for brooding and rearing chicks and broilers is the deep litter, for the simple reason that battery cage is designed essentially for adult birds. Nevertheless, it has been reported that chicks tend to grow faster when reared in cages than on deep litter due to:

- Reduced social conflicts when kept in the battery cage.
- Stress caused by wire floors.
- Avoidance of direct contact with feacal droppings.

Broilers may develop breast blisters in cages thus reducing the quality of their carcass.

Other management factors necessary to meet the requirements of the fowls as they grow older are:

6. **Debeaking:** This involves partial removal of the beak to prevent vice habits such as pecking, feather-pulling, cannibalism and egg-eating depending on the age these occur. While debeaking of birds can take place at 3-5 weeks, the birds should be debeaked latest between 15-17 weeks of age. Debeaking is done to control or solve these problems because they are indices of management defects like inadequate feeding and drinking, inadequate floor spaces, imbalanced diet, stress. Debeaking should be performed in the morning in hot weather to minimize bleeding. A higher level of vitamin K may be fed before debeaking to accelerate clotting. Debeaking can be done using a pair of scissors or an electric debeaker. If the former is used to cut the beaks, the raw surface should be rubbed with caustic potash to minimize bleeding which normally is excessive. The electric debeaker on the other

hand cuts the beak and simultaneously cauterizes the raw surface and thereby stops or minimizes bleeding.

7.   **Despurring:** The spur is an extra digit of the male which in light breeds is well developed. This causes wounds on the back of breeding hens when mating and may reduce fertility as breeding hens avoid mating. The spur is removed at 10-16 weeks when the cap is well formed with a sharp knife or a pair of scissors.

8.   **Transfer of Birds:** In modern poultry operations, the female birds may become layers and stay in the housing until they become spent layers in the housing. This is referred to as the single stage intensive system. Movement from one house to another at specific stages of growth is called a multi stage intensive system. If growers are to be transferred to a different house for laying, this should be done at between 16-18 weeks before the birds begin to lay eggs. Transfer of birds should be done using crates and preferably early in the morning to avoid the birds becoming stressed.

4.0   CONCLUSION

This unit has exposed you to the practical significance of rearing chicks from the end of chicks phase to point of lay for the overall success of the poultry industry. You should be thus equipped to manage birds generally described as growers by providing for them appropriate housing, facilities, feed and space.

5.0   SUMMARY

This unit has dealt with the following:

- The definition of rearing and its importance to the overall concept of chicken production.
- Critical factors in the construction of a poultry house.
- Equipment like feeding and watering troughs, their sizes and shapes.
- Important elements in rearing like ventilation, temperature, light, type of diet, preferred management system, debeaking, despurring, and movement of birds.

6.0   ASSIGNMENT

1.   Define rearing.
2.   Enumerate the factors you would consider when constructing a poultry house.
3.   Mention the steps required when rearing birds.
4.   What is the difference between feeding troughs and waterers used for brooding and the ones used at the grower phase ?

5.   Make a list of the miscellaneous equipment required on a poultry farm.

7.0   REFERENCES

Banerjee, G.C. (1976). *Poultry*. New Delhi: Oxford & IBH
     Publishing Co., PVT Ltd.

Oluyemi, J. A. and Roberts, F.A. (2000). *Poultry Production in
     Warm Wet Climates*. Ibadan: Spectrum Books Ltd.

UNIT 3   PRODUCTION OF EGG AND BROILER

CONTENTS

1.0   Introduction
2.0   Objectives
3.0   Main Content
        Laying
    3.1   Birds
                Indices for Evaluating the Performance of the
            3.1.1 Layer
            3.1.2 The Egg Producing Cycle
            3.1.3 Factors Affecting the Performance of the Layer
    3.2   Management of Layers
            3.2.1 Routine Operations
            3.2.2 Specific Operations
    3.3   Management of Breeders
    3.4   Broiler (Table Bird) Production
            3.4.1 Facts Pertinent to an Understanding of Broiler
                  Production
            3.4.2 Breeds of Broilers
            3.4.3 Broiler Housing
            3.4.4 Management Practices for Broilers
4.0   Conclusion
5.0   Summary
6.0   Assignment
7.0   References

1.0   INTRODUCTION

Poultry meat and egg for human consumption are the two reasons for raising broilers and pullet chicks. It has generally been agreed that poultry is a sub sector in the livestock industry necessary to bridge the gap between demand and supply of animal protein within the shortest possible time. However, the skill of the poultry farmer in raising these poultry species is vital to an efficient and profitable enterprise. A result-oriented poultry enterprise requires good poultry management which involves a good knowledge of feeding, housing, diseases, record keeping, breeds and breeding, vaccination, use of medication and the implication of natural and artificial lights on birds. This shows that it takes a lot of technical know-how in many different fields. This unit therefore addresses production and management issues relating to table meat and eggs.

2.0   OBJECTIVES

This unit is packaged to enable you:

- identify and explain the steps involved in producing table eggs and meat
- explain the risks involved in keeping broiler and pullet chicks if management practices are neglected
- identify and explain the variables for the evaluation of performance of broilers and pullets.

3.0   MAIN CONTENT

3.1   Laying Birds

A laying hen will produce eggs for a number of years, but it is only economical to keep the layers up to 18 months i.e. after one year in lay; the adult fowl is either a layer or a breeder. The latter comprises males and females for producing fertile eggs. Egg production strains are usually separated into males and females at day old before sale. Be sure to place order for only the females of these types of birds. Their male counterparts are called cockerels and they grow slowly and may not be economical to keep for meat production. If part of the table egg production objective is to hatch eggs from the flock, then the farmer may request for not more than 10% of these egg production type birds as males.

The level of performance of the layer under optimum feeding and management depends largely on the genetic capability of the birds and their health status at hatching time. The producer must then exercise caution to buy only breeds that have been known to do well in his environment and also to purchase them from a reliable hatchery. There is no perfect breed of chickens. Each has its advantages and disadvantages. A poultry farmer then settles for the breed that will give him the greatest number of desirable characteristics that he wants with less of the undesirable characteristics. Breeds that are prevalent under tropical conditions are the Rhode Island Red, New Hampshire, Plymouth Rock and Australorp. These are heavy breeds. Among the light breeds, the most poplar is the white leghorn, which is known to be heat-tolerant. The Rhode Island Red is one breed that has been developed as a dual purpose bird.

3.1.1 Indices for Evaluating the Performance of the Layer

These indices are:

1. **Egg Production or Number of Eggs Laid**: This is the major index of performance of the commercial layer. It accounts for about 90% of the income in egg production. The egg production cycle shows that the maximum number of eggs that a fowl can produce in its first year in lay (i.e pullet year) is about 300 eggs. It is not common for birds to attain and they rarely exceed this level. The rate of egg production in a first stage is often expressed as:

a) Hen-day egg production = $\dfrac{\text{Average daily egg production x 100}}{\text{Average daily number of birds alive}}$

Or

b) Hen-housed egg production = $\dfrac{\text{Average daily egg production x 100}}{\text{No. of birds housed at the start of lay}}$

In commercial enterprise, hen-housed egg production is more commonly used.

2. **Egg size**: This is an egg quality parameter. It varies with age and strain of birds. Average egg size increases from about 36gms at point of lay (about 24 weeks of age) to about 58gms at 42 weeks of age. Egg size appears to increase throughout the pullet years. Eggs are heavier in the temperate regions. The following factors have negative effect on egg size:

a) Unbalanced state or badly mixed feed
b) Feed restriction
c) Lack of clean, cool fresh water
d) Rations containing less than 15% protein
e) High laying house temperature
f) Disease
g) Early maturity of fowl
h) Age of birds (this is just before birds stop laying).

3. **Egg Shell Thickness:** This is another egg quality parameter of economic importance. Average shell thickness of the

fowl is about 0.34mm. The thinner the shell, the higher the percentage of cracks which will lower revenue.

4.   **Shell Colour:** Though this is not of any nutritional importance, brown shelled eggs are normally preferred by consumers.

5.   **Yolk Colour:** This is also not of any nutritional value. However, bright or deep yellow yolk is preferred to white.

6.   **Feed Efficiency:** This is a measure of how efficiently a given feed is being converted into products. The better the quality of the feed, the better its rate of conversion into eggs.

$$\text{Feed efficiency} = \frac{\text{Feed consumed}}{\text{Kg of eggs produced}}$$

7.   **Mortality**: It is expressed as:

$$\text{Mortality} = \frac{\text{No. of birds dead} \times 100}{\text{No. of birds started.}}$$

For laying birds the mortality rate should be about 10% throughout the laying period. Increase in mortality may be an indication of a disease outbreak. The services of a veterinarian may be needed.

3.1.2 Egg Producing Cycle

The age at point of lay (POL) is between 22-24 weeks of age depending on the breed. Light breeds begin to lay first. The end of lay (EOL) is a year or two after point of lay. However, layers are culled after one year in lay i.e. at 18 months of age. When egg production starts, it reaches a peak (about 80%) at about 42 weeks of age. This marks the end of the first phase of the pullet year laying cycle and the start of the second phase (43- 62 weeks of age) during which there is a gradual fall in production to about 65%. After this, the pullet enters into the third phase of its first year in lay which is up to 72 weeks. This phase terminates in the moulting of the fowl. Egg production becomes practically nil.

3.1.3   Factors Affecting the Performance of the Layer

1.   **Temperature:** Hens need a moderate temperature for optimal performance. The thermo neutral zones of the adult fowl within which performance is not adversely

affected by temperature is from 12.8°C to 26.0°C. This temperature range supports the highest egg qualities. When temperatures fall below the thermo neutral zone, feed consumption increases while egg production drops and shell thickness is reduced. Temperatures higher than 26.0°C as in the tropics depress egg yield and egg qualities.

2. **Relative Humidity:** High relative humidity (RH) impedes evaporative cooling and therefore makes panting virtually ineffective. This aggravates thermal stress. High RH may increase the risk of wet and mouldy litter. The recommended RH is 50-80% for layers.

3. **Ventilation:** The fowl is a small animal with a rapid metabolism hence its air requirements per unit of body is high compared with that of other animals. The requirement can be met by straight-through passive ventilation in the hen houses. A good ventilation is also needed to purify the air of carbon dioxide, ammonia and noxious gases. The fowl can withstand a high rate of air movement, especially when the temperature is high because of its cooling effect.

4. **Light:** Light has been shown to stimulate egg production in all birds and chicken is no exception. This is achieved by stimulating the pituitary gland which releases certain hormones necessary for ovulation. The process requires couple of hours for completion of the job up to egg laying. Increasing day light advances sexual maturity and vice versa. Precocious maturity tend to result in a depressed rate of lay, and reduced egg size because of low POL body weight, light requirement considered enough for production is about 10 lux (one foot candle). The use of artificial light to give 14 to 16 hours light period helps to overcome the problem with natural day length which varies with seasons. The standard practice is to place one ceiling outlet for each $18.6m^2$ of floor and artificial lights should first be used on pullets after 5 months of age by giving 1 hour additional light to the day light.

5. **Noise:** Intermittent noise impacts negatively on egg production. A continuous noise however, neutralizes the shock effect of sudden noises.

6. **Floor, Feeding and Drinking Space:** These factors interact with temperature, ventilation, RH to affect the performance of the fowl. It is therefore important to adhere to the

established floor, feeding ad drinking space requirements per bird.

3.2 Management of Layers

Layers, like chicks and growers are taken care of by applying some routine operations daily and by performing some specific operations as the need for them arise. Layers are raised in the laying house which should have been stopping de-wormed at least 3 weeks before transfer, before released eggs would reach the effective stage and cause re-infection. The birds should also be deloused only a few days to their transfer. Crates are needed to move the birds during the coolest part of the day and this should involve two or three persons. The birds should not be handled roughly. When deep litter is used, well made nests of the correct number should be fixed.

3.2.1 Routine Operations

1. Dead birds are removed once found to prevent contamination of the live birds.
2. Fresh feed is added to stale feed in the feeder and mixed after the litter and droppings in the latter have been removed. A feed depth of not more than one-half is recommended and feed given ad libitum.
3. Waterers are taken out, cleaned and re-filled with clean, cool water.
4. Eggs are collected at 9am, 12 noon and 4pm.
5. The litter should be turned by using a rake.

If a battery cage is used and birds are in separate compartments, the drinking trough should first be cleaned removing the stale water and then refilled. Fresh feed is added to the stale one in the feeding trough and mixed up. Dead birds should then be removed.

3.2.2 Specific Operations

These operations help to avert situations that may lower the performance of the birds. These operations include:

1. **Culling:** This is the continual elimination of undesirable birds from the flock. This may be due to poor performance broodiness, vice habits, deformities, illness. However, layers are culled primarily on the basis of their ability to lay eggs. Fowls in production can be identified outwardly if their combs are large and bright, eyes are bright and alert, beaks are not parrot-like and their heads not narrow.

2.   **Control of Vice Habits:** Any vice habit observed is an indicator of a stress factor. Vice habits may be due to:

a)   Inadequate space heading to struggle for survival
b)   Nutritionally deficient diet particularly methionine causing pecking
c)   The light being too bright which may cause nervousness which results in pecking.

3.   **Controlling** Egg Defects: Egg defects include abnormal egg size, soft-shelled eggs and a high percentage of eggs with cracks. Egg size tends to increase from POL to just before birds stop to lay. However small egg sizes may be caused by the deficiency of amino and essential fatty acid like dietary linoleic acid. Shellless eggs may occur once in a while if the eggs spend a shorter time in the uterus, or the situation may be caused by diseases like pullorum, Newcastle disease and bronchitis. A high percentage of cracks is an indication of calcium deficiency or of vitamins A and D or the unbalance of nutrients. It may also be due to poor management like inadequate nesting facilities or hard floored nests and infrequent egg collection. To avoid dirty eggs, they should be collected regularly and the nest floor should be covered with dry, clean litter.

4.   **Handling Poultry Manure:** The commercialization of poultry production has now made poultry manure to constitute an environmental problem rather than an asset. Because it is moist and because of its content of nutrient and organic matter, the manure is a suitable breeding ground for pestiferous flies like house flies. The manure is often a source of odour caused by the production of fatty acids like butyric, valeric and caprylic acids.
Flies can be controlled by spraying droppings with insecticides and larvicide's. A form of biological control is the use of insects to prey on the larvae of the flies. Poultry manure can be disposed of by using it for gardening; it can be composted, incinerated, used for gas production or as feed for livestock. Poultry droppings are removed periodically depending on their quantity and/or condition. Also poultry litter is removed before it poses a health hazard to the birds and fresh wood shavings are used to replace the old one.

The wood shaving should be raked with the droppings to keep it dry and free from flies. Incidences of wet litter occur and may be due to management errors like including too much salt in feed (this has a laxative effect), water spillage, over filled water troughs and seepage of underground water.

5. **Handling Cage Fatigue:** Some prolific layers and at peak of laying, some birds may suffer leg weakness which makes them to squat, unable to reach feed and water and eventually starve to death. Cage fatigued is not remedied with medication but by releasing the birds from their cages onto floor litter where there is room for physical exercise. Grasses can also be harvested, washed and put in the house for them to eat.

6. **Moulting:** This is the process of shedding and renewing feathers; it occurs normally once a year, though it may occur in certain individuals twice a year and more rarely, only once in a period of two years. Hens usually moult in the following order: head, neck, body (breast, back and abdomen), wing and tail. Birds can be force-moulted by stress and by drug treatment. Birds force-moulted may produce more eggs, or eggs that are larger, have larger yolk at the expense of the albumen, higher haugh unit, and thicker shells while the birds have larger end-of-lay body weight.

The specific effect produced depends on:

a) the period after point of lay when treatment is applied
b) whether treatment consists of drug therapy or stress due to starvation and
c) the duration of the moult.

It is considered necessary to force-moult when replacement birds are not readily available, if the flock shows a decline in haugh unit to 72 and shell thickness to 0.3mm, if there is a premium for extra large eggs and there is prices of egg are good.

7. **Egg-eating:** This starts in a flock usually by one or a few birds but soon rapidly spreads. Accidental breakage of eggs, soft-shelled eggs and infrequent collection of eggs may prompt birds into this habit. Other possible causes are nutritional imbalance and inadequate nesting facilities.

8. **Heat Stress Management:** Heat stress is a great economic threat to the poultry industry. Adverse effects of heat stress include depression in egg production, egg weight, shell thickness, feed intake, feed efficiency, fertility in the male, hatchability, growth rate. A well ventilated poultry house helps greatly to combat thermal stress. Strains of the chicken differ genetically in their ability to resist heat stress, either in terms of survival rate or of laying performance.

The White Leghorn appears to be the best in terms of laying performance. Resistance to thermal stress can be developed. A bird exposed to a warm climate for a certain period has its thermo-regulatory mechanism altered. Because of reduced feed intake of the fowl under thermal stress, the bird then consumes less nutrients to support satisfactory levels of production. Thus, a part of heat stress management will be to increase the dietary nutrients density. Dietary energy should be so increased as to cause fatness which aggravates heat stress in layers. Some drugs help to induce resistance to heat stress e.g. tranquilizers like reserpine and sympathetic agents like morphine. Physical measures to combat heat stress include a continuous supply of cool water to the birds.

3.3 Management of Breeders

Breeders are managed essentially using the same techniques that are applicable to layers. The minor differences in practical details rest on the assumption that the breeders require more physical stamina and fitness to perform satisfactorily as breeders. This is achieved through feeding and physical exercises. The following are critical issues:

1. In the growers phase, their diets are such that will prevent fatness in the adult breeders.
2. They are reared on floor to give opportunity for physical exercise.
3. They are given more floor space, and more feeding and water space.
4. To prevent precocious mating, males and females are managed separately till maturity.
5. While artificial insemination is possible, it is not considered necessary in poultry. This is because of the high efficiency of the cocks as breeders and partly because of the poor storage qualities of semen and its lack of a suitable dilutent. Efficiency of the cock is reduced by the frequency of mating and thus the male to female ratio should not be higher than the recommended rate. The number of female should also not be too small as this promotes fighting

among the females. For pen mating the ratio is one male to 3 or 4 females per pen. In case of flock mating, one male to 8 females for large strain or to 10 females for light strain.

6. The males are introduced into the female flock about 6 weeks after point of lay of the pullets. By this time the pullet breeders must have reached the egg size suitable for setting.

7. To obtain good quality eggs, the nesting facilities should be adequate and clean, and there should be frequent egg collection.

8. When feeding, cocks would normally prefer the females and this results in their being under fed. (They need to be well fed for optimum performance.)Thus, some feeders should be set higher than others exclusively for the males.

3.4 Broiler (Table Birds) Production

Broilers are fast growing birds which reach market weight of 1.6kg to 2kg in 8-10 weeks or 12 weeks at most. A broiler or fryer can be of either sex. Its flesh is tender, with soft pliable smooth textured and flexible breast. The commercial tale birds industry is now largely based on broilers. The other types of table birds are either:

- The by-products of egg production i.e. spent layers or
- The by-products of hatchery operations like poussins, roasters.

3.4.1 Facts Pertinent to an Understanding of Broiler Performance

1. At any given age, males are heavier than females.
2. Weekly increases in body weight are not uniform and weight gains increase until reaching a maximum at about the eighth week for straight-run (both sexes together).
3. Weekly feed consumption increases as weight increases.
4. The more feed consumed, the better the feed conversion at a given age.
5. As weekly gains increase, feed efficiency increases.
6. Healthy birds consume more feed and have better feed conversion than sick birds.
7. The greater the activity of broilers, the lower the feed efficiency.
8. Cannibalism causes lowered feed intake, growth and feed conversion.
9. Changes in temperature cause changes in feed consumption. High temperatures reduce feed intake while low temperatures cause them to eat more.
10. At market time, the birds in a flock will not be uniform in weight.
11. Mortality rate should not exceed 5%.

3.4.2 Breeds of Broilers

Commercial hybrid broiler chicks are derived from Plymouth Rock, Cornix Sussex, and Rhode Island Red. Progeny test and family selection have been effective in the development of broiler lines. The end product of all well-planned selected crosses is to produce a modern chick, white in color, yellow shanked, which grows faster than either of the parents (hybrid vigour), with tender flesh and flexible breast cartilage. All these characteristics of broilers depend on the genetic make up of their parents which themselves are not broilers.

3.4.3 Broiler Housing

Broilers are reared traditionally on deep litter. In modern commercial broiler production, the bird spends its entire life in one house. This means that broilers are not brooded in a special brooder house, then moved to another house for growing. Broiler raising is essentially, a brooding operation. The broiler house should be located in such a way that:

1. It takes advantage of prevailing wind for ventilation and sun for light.
2. Its ground elevation is higher than the surrounding ground level to permit good water drainage away from building and
3. It is readily accessible to power and water supply.

    There are many different styles and designs of houses and even more variations in equipment. What is important is that broiler houses and equipment provide comfortable conditions, so that the birds can perform at the highest level of which they are genetically capable. A satisfactory broiler house must protect the birds against heat and cold, high winds and inclement weather.

3.4.4 Management Practices for Broilers

The essential conditions for broiler rearing are similar to that of the pullet chicks that they have been discussed. However, the following should be noted:

- **Poultry House Temperature:** Broiler chicks require a higher starting temperature of about 35°C which is gradually reduced to environmental temperature.

- **Ventilation of Broiler House:** A higher rate of ventilation is required in the house because broilers have a higher stocking density than pullet chicks. The main functions of ventilation are to maintain O_2, keep CO_2 at low level, remove dust or moisture and ammonia from the house and maintain required temperature. In the tropics the house should be free of internal fittings and partitions that may impede straight-through ventilation.

- **Lighting for Broilers:** Many operators use all night lights during early growing period. A low light intensity of 1.076 lux or less is adequate for broilers after an initial light intensity of about 10.76 lux necessary for the first few days. The birds require only enough light to see the feed.

- **Broiler Feeds:** Broilers require higher levels of certain nutrients like protein with the amino acids and energy than pullet chicks. Starter ration is having more protein about 22% and less metabolisable energy 2,900Kcal than the finisher ration, about 20% and 3000 Kcal ME/kg. The finisher diet containing increased levels of fat and xanthophylls pigments aids in the development of the uniform yellow skin colour.

- **Sexing:** Broilers may be sexed by vent, colour or rate of feathering. Males attain market weight faster than females of the same age. The latter grow more slowly and need less protein than males. Males convert feed to meat more efficiently than females. Females also show less response to chemical growth promoters than males.

- **Floor Space Requirement:** Broilers require a floor space of $0.06m^2$ from day old to market age. This stocking rate is mainly to ensure maximum profit from floor space and also to restrict extensive movement which is accompanied by the wasteful dissipation of energy by the birds.

- **Broiler Health Programme:** A health programme is fundamental to successful broiler production. A suggested disease prevention and control programme is as follows:

  - Start with disease-free chicks
  - Use effective drugs and vaccines
  - Keep feed free from aflatoxin
  - Only people wearing disinfected boots and clean clothing should be allowed into broiler house
  - If there is more than one age group on the farm, the younger batch should be attended to first while performing daily routine works.
  - Cover floor with clean litter at least 5cm deep after each clean out.
  - Debeaking: In addition to preventing cannibalism, debeaking lessens mash feed wastage. Chicks are debeaked at one day old. However, if management is standard, the feed is adequate and well balanced and the light is dim, it may not be essential.

4.0　CONCLUSION

This unit has been shown very clearly the differences and similarities in raising chickens for table egg and meat, and the breeds of chickens most suitable for each enterprise. Furthermore the management of breeders has been discussed for sustainable poultry development.

5.0　SUMMARY

This unit explains the following:

- The need to place order for environmentally friendly breeds of birds from a reliable hatchery
- Breeds of laying birds and broilers
- Indices for evaluating the performance of the layer, egg production cycle, factors affecting the performance of the layer
- Management of layers, breeders and broilers, and the required routine and specific operations
- Facts pertinent to an understanding of broiler performance
- Broiler housing.

6.0   ASSIGNMENT

1. Mention the breeds of laying hens and broilers common in the tropics.
2. Enumerate the criteria commonly used to evaluate the performance of the layer.
3   a. At what age does a pullet attain the point of lay? b. At what age does a broiler attain market weight?
4. List the management practices for broilers.
5. What is the difference between hen-day egg production and hen-housed egg production?
6. How would you calculate mortality rate on a poultry farm?

7.0   REFERENCES

Banerjee, G.C. (1976). *Poultry*. New Delhi: Oxford and IBH Publishing Co. PVT Ltd.

Oluyemi, J. A. and Roberts, F.A. (2000). *Poultry Production in Warm Wet Climates*. Ibadan: Spectrum Books Ltd.

Wong, G. *Broiler Production for the South Pacific*. A Teacher's Guide.
CTA. Lome Convention.

UNIT 4   PROCESSING AND MARKETING OF POULTRY AND POULTRY PRODUCTS

CONTENTS

Introductio
1.0   n
2.0   Objectives
3.0   Main Content
          Egg
3.1   handling
          3.1.1 Egg Cleaning
          3.1.2 Egg Preservation/Storage
          3.1.3 Egg Grading
3.2   Marketing Eggs
3.3   Poultry Meat
          3.3.1 Processing of Chicken
                  3.3.1.1 Catching and Transportation
                  3.3.1.2 Slaughtering
                  3.3.1.3 Plucking
                  3.3.1.4 Evisceration/Carcass Preparation
                  3.3.1.5 Preservation
                  3.3.1.6 Storage
          3.3.2 Spoilage of Poultry Meat
                  3.3.2.1 Factors Favouring the Survival of Organisms
                  3.3.2.2 Measures against the Spoilage of Poultry Meat
          3.3.3 Marketing of Poultry Meat
4.0   Conclusion
5.0   Summary
6.0   Assignment
7.0   References

1.0   INTRODUCTION

The main poultry products marketed in most countries are eggs and poultry meat. The tastes of consumers vary and for acceptability of these products to the consuming public, prompt disposal is important to avoid deterioration and/or spoilage and to make the enterprise profitable. It is therefore not only important for farmers to think in terms of production for the purposes of bridging the protein gap in the country, but the handling of these major products of the industry in terms of processing and marketing is equally important. This involves some technicalities which this unit will address.

2.0   OBJECTIVES

At the end of this unit you should be able to:

- explain egg grading and packaging
- explain the stages involved in processing poultry meat
- explain the storage of eggs and poultry meat before sales
- expressly state how to market poultry eggs and meat.

3.0   MAIN CONTENT

3.1   Egg handling

The following are ideal ways of handling eggs:

3.1.1 Egg Cleaning

Eggs are a very rich source of animal protein. However, they are a good medium for bacteria and thus can easily become infected and lose their quality if incorrectly handled after being laid. It is therefore, important that eggs should be produced in as clean a form as possible to avoid spoilage and to avoid the need to wash them which can remove the protective coat from the outside of the egg. Dirty eggs should be cleaned with abrasive materials in preference to washing. If it is necessary to wash, the best method is by immersion between 33_oC and 35_oC in temperate climates and 40^oC in the tropics. The immersion time varies with temperature. At lower temperature immersion time of 10-15 minutes is necessary but at higher temperature immersion time of 3-5 minutes is adequate. The amount of sanitizer put into the water should be as advised by the manufacturers. Water used for cleaning should be changed frequently to minimize the risk of contamination and washed eggs should not be stored.

3.1.2 Egg Preservation/Storage

Sometimes, the poultry farmer experiences egg glut and since eggs can very quickly deteriorate, it is important to know how to preserve them. Egg preservation is to minimize the loss of moisture and carbon-dioxide which forms the starting point of deteriorative changes. The ideal temperature for storage is lower than 13₀C which is often impossible in tropical countries. Thus in these countries, the eggs should be kept out of direct sunlight and put in the coolest place possible and sold by the third day after laying. Eggs absorb strong odours very quickly and should therefore be stored in places where such odours are absent. Generally, refrigeration rather than evaporative cooling should be preferred in the tropics. Some methods for preserving eggs are as follows:

1. **The Water Glass Method:** This involves dipping eggs in a solution of sodium silicate or water glass. A coating of silica is formed over the shells and their pores are completely closed. By this method eggs can be stored safely for up to 6 months. About 15 dozen eggs can be preserved in 10 litres of the solution.

2. **The Lime Water Method:** This involves dipping eggs in the supernatant liquid (lime water) obtained by adding 1kg of unslaked lime to 20 litres of water in an enamel vessel. Eggs can be preserved this way for nearly six months.

3. **Oil Protection:** Eggs are dipped in warm oil 4-6 hours after lay. The oil temperature should be 11°C higher than that of the egg. The oil should be colourless, tasteless and odourless e.g. coconut, groundnut oils. The oil seals the pores of the shell which prevents evaporation and loss of carbon dioxide, thus it maintains good internal quality and prevents weight loss. Before re-use, the oil is heated to 116₀C to kill spoilage bacteria, and it is filtered. Four litres of oil is sufficient for 30 cases of eggs.

4. **Thermostabilization:** This is the stabilization of egg quality by heat. Eggs may be thermostabilized by immersing the shell eggs for 15 minutes in water at 54.40°C or at 60°C for 3 to 5 minutes. This process helps to pasteurize the eggs (kills bacteria on the egg shell), de-fertilizes the eggs and stabilizes the egg.

5. **Cold Storage:** The temperature of an egg-storage room should be maintained at +0.5₀C to -0.5₀C and relative humidity of 75 to 85%.

6. **Freezing:** The freezing of the internal contents of eggs is a common method of preservation especially in the

developed countries. The equipment for freezing liquid egg consists of a candler, eggs washer, breaking table or machine, churn, scale, tables and cleaning tanks and racks. The eggs are first candled to detect any possible defects. Before breaking, eggs should be washed with water at 11°C higher than the temperature of the egg using an odourless, germicidal, colourless and non-toxic detergent sanitizer. The yolk and the white may be frozen separately with addition of 5% glycerine. The egg contents are then frozen in a freezer at a low temperature of about - 41°C. The contents are kept at a low temperature until required for use.

7. **Drying:** Egg drying is now being used in place of freezing. The egg contents are dried at a temperature of 160₀F and stored under 50°F to convert white, yolk or the whole egg into a fine powder.With the present day, low egg production and unsatisfactory marketing facilities, preservation and storing of eggs by freezing and drying may not be of immediate interest in Nigeria.

3.1.3 Egg Grading

Grading is the sorting out of eggs into different categories according to their individual weight, shell shape and interior quality. Only eggs with smooth shells and normal shape are sent to market. In most countries where eggs are in short supply, grading is not necessary except if it will guarantee an increased income because grading takes time and costs money.

Based on the quality of eggs and according to size, four classes have been adopted. Grading for internal quality is done by candling while for weight of an individual egg there are various types of automatic devices in the market. Egg grading according to size is as follows:

Table 3.4:   Standards for Weight Classification of Shell Eggs

Size	Weight per Egg (g)
Extra large	≥60
Large	53–69
Medium	45–52
Small	38–44

3.2   Marketing Eggs

In developing countries, where egg production is low, eggs are easily packaged and distributed without any preparation before consumption apart from cooking the product in one way or another. In some countries, populations will not consume fertilized eggs-whereas in other countries, fertilized eggs are preferred. These preferences should be considered when eggs are being prepared for sale. To maximize income, an egg farmer must ensure that his maximum supply of egg coincides with the minimum supply of eggs from local sources. With rapid expansion in the poultry industry, it is very easy to go from a deficit to a surplus supply and if large amounts of capital are put into poultry production, it would be easy for farmers producing these eggs to go bankrupt. Therefore, a careful assessment of the likely market, the changing market and changes in other farmers' levels of production should be put into consideration before committing large capital on developing poultry units.

3.3   Poultry Meat

This can be a product of either a dual-purpose poultry farm that produces both meat and eggs and or a single-purpose poultry farm which produces either meat or eggs for human consumption. Poultry meat provides man with nutrients for growth, tissue replacement and for weight control because of its lower fat content. Poultry meat contains more unsaturated fatty acids than red meat. The fat content of chicken is higher in males and in the older chickens. Most fat in poultry meat is found under the skin and not distributed throughout the tissues. The protein in poultry meat is similar to that of beef and pork in amino acids and it contains all the essential amino acids required by man. The protein is easily digested. Poultry meat is also a good source of riboflavin, thiamin and ascorbic acid. Minerals present in the meat include, sodium, iron, sulphur, calcium, phosphorus and chlorine.

3.3.1 Processing of Chicken

The processing of chicken is the sequence of treatments to which the chicken is subjected to in order to obtain poultry meat for cooking. All birds destined to be slaughtered should be fasted for the previous 4-6 hours to allow the intestine to be emptied. This helps to improve tenderness. If the poultry are not starved before slaughter, the gut may rapture when the carcass is eviscerated and its content will contaminate the carcass.

3.3.1.1 Catching and Transportation

Chickens can be marketed as chicken or slaughtered and prepared for the table. Either way the birds should be caught under the least stressful conditions. The catching should be by grasping them by shanks with no more than 4 or 5 being carried at a time. Under tropical or subtropical conditions, the best solution may be to catch the birds at dusk or at night and put them in transportation crates, head first. These crates should have dimensions of 80cm x 60cm x 30cm and will hold ten mature broilers or adult laying birds. Birds in crates should be kept out of the sun but in a well ventilated place. Also birds in crates should not be transported during the heat of the day.

3.3.1.2 Slaughtering

It is a standard practice to slaughter chickens at the correct age to avoid
(a)   wastage of chicken feed and money because feed used by
mature chickens after the 8th or 9th week is uneconomical and (b)
accumulation of excess fat and loss of quality or tenderness of the
meat which is not acceptable to most consumers.

The method of killing adopted influences the extent of blood drainage from the carcass. Good drainage is desirable if the carcass is to be stored for long. Some methods of slaughtering poultry are:

1.   To immobilize the chicken in a bleeding cone and to cut the jugular vein to ensure complete exsanguinations. The cut can be made below the ear.
2.   To stun the birds by passing their heads through a shallow trough of electrified water. This is done in large scale slaughtering. Once the birds are stunned, they are slaughtered by cutting the jugular vein with a knife.
3.   To hold the chickens by their legs and make a clean cut through the veins in the neck with a sharp knife about 2cm below the eyes. In all methods, allow the blood to drain away into a container rather than spilling around the slaughter house.

3.3.1.3 Plucking

This is the removal of the feathers. The following methods can be used:

1.   **Scalding:** This is the immersion of birds in hot water for about two minutes after killing. The temperature of the hot water is about 52°C for broilers, 55°C for old laying hens and 59°C for turkey. Immersion helps to relax muscles and make them soft, allowing the feathers to be plucked easily.

2.   **Dry Plucking:** The feathers are removed by hand easily soon after slaughter when the body is warm. The chicken is held head-

downwards with one hand and the feathers are removed with the other hand. It should be done starting from the large feathers, followed by the back, sides and the abdomen, the breast feathers, the legs, neck and wings.

3. **The use of Mechanical Pluckers:** With these machines the feathers are removed by the action of rubber fingers mounted on rapidly revolving drums. The quill feathers are removed by hand. This method can be adopted by farmers producing on a large scale.

3.3.1.4 Evisceration/Carcass Preparation

Cut open the chickens by cutting around the vent/anus area to remove the internal organs. Remove the gut and separate edible parts like the gizzard, heart and liver from the rest.

Further, cut open the gizzard and remove the waste and the skin layer known as the epithelium enclosing the undigested feed. The giblets consists of the heart, gizzard and liver which with the neck may or may not be included as part of the carcass. The shanks are removed. The chickens are thoroughly washed before the rest of the operations are carried out. The chickens should be hanged up for about 5-10 minutes to drain excess water then wrap them with wrapping plastic bags. The weights of the chickens are taken and they are graded according to market specifications based on market requirements.

3.3.1.5 Preservation

Most of the carcass preparation is carried out at normal body temperatures. However, thereafter, the carcasses should be cooled as soon as possible to limit the extent bacterial growth. A satisfactory method of chilling the carcasses is in a refrigeration plant, if possible one that uses a forced draught. The incoming air needs to have its moisture content closely controlled to avoid excessive moisture loss from the carcasses.

3.3.1.6 Storage

The temperature at which the carcasses are stored is dependent to a degree on the length of time for which the carcasses are to be stored. If they are to be consumed within a day or two, they can be stored in a refrigerator at $+2^{\circ}C$. If they are to be stored for a long period of time, they should be frozen to $-5^{\circ}C$ or even to $-18^{\circ}C$.

3.3.2 Spoilage of Poultry Meat

Poultry meat can deteriorate if hygienic conditions are not maintained in the processing line. Though the muscle tissue of a healthy bird is sterile, the bird carries millions of different types of organisms on feathers, feet and intestinal tract.

3.3.2.1 Factors Favouring the Survival of Organisms

1.   The presence of large numbers of them on the carcass.
2.   Spore formation as in poisoning and spoilage organism (clostridium perfigens)
3.   A double source of infection from Salmonella spp and E.coli which are present on the farm and in the intestine of the fowl.
4.   Optimum temperature – The food poisoning organisms known as mesophills multiply rapidly at body temperature but slowly at 10_oC and 15_oC.

3.3.2.2 Measures against the Spoilage of Poultry Meat

1.   **Chlorination:** This involves the carcass being treated with sterile water. Addition of chlorine or sodium hypochlorite to water makes it to have a very low bactericidal activity.

2.   **Cold Storage:** For a short period of cold storage, the birds may not be eviscerated, wrapped individually or even bled. The chicken is chilled at 4^oC immediately after slaughter. For long storage life basic requirements include sanitary processing, rapid chilling, low storage temperature and moisture – proof packaging. The chickens are stored at -18_oC. If stored at 7_oC, storage life will only last for a few days.

3.3.2 Marketing of Poultry Meat

Marketing means selling broiler chickens for money. The farmer has to decide whether or not he will market the meat as live birds or will slaughter and prepare the birds for the table. This decision will depend on factors like:

1.   The sophistication of the markets
2.   The religious beliefs of the consumers
3.   The pattern of consumption.

There are two main types of markets which are:

a)   Contracted markets: These are those that have a verbal or nonverbal agreement between the producer and the buyer with specific terms and conditions as to what to buy and sell. Examples of this market type are hotels, hostels, supermarkets, institutions and commercial slaughter houses.

b)   Non-contracted markets: These are also known as free or open markets because the farmer is not bound by any agreement to sell to anybody. Chickens can be sold live or after being slaughtered. Examples are home consumption, close friends and relatives, roadside traders, farm gate, local farmers' market and retail outlets.

4.0   CONCLUSION

Poultry table egg and meat which are the primary products that are obtained from the poultry industry, for the purposes of bridging the protein gap between the demand for animal protein in human diet and its supply need proper handling to avoid deterioration and/or spoilage in order to make the enterprise profitable.

5.0   SUMMARY

This unit has dealt with:

- The various constituents of egg handling (egg cleaning, egg preservation and egg grading)
- The considerations which help the farmer to decide on his marketing strategies for table egg and meat
- The steps necessary for processing chicken to obtain poultry meat for human consumption
- The measures against spoilage.

6.0   ASSIGNMENT

1.   Why must eggs for human consumption or for hatching be clean?
2.   Justify the need for egg preservation and list the methods for achieving this.
3.   Mention the steps required for processing chicken.
3.   List the types of market available for poultry meat.
4.   Define egg grading.
5.   What can cause spoilage of poultry meat?

7.0   REFERENCES

Banerjee, G.C. (1976). *Poultry*. 3rd (ed). New Delhi: Oxford and IBH Publishing Co., PVT Ltd.

Oluyemi, J.A and Roberts, F.A (2000). *Poultry Production in Warm Wet Climates*. Ibadan: Spectrum Books Ltd.

Smith, A. J. (1990). *Poultry. The Tropical Agriculturist*. London & Basingstoke: Macmillan Education Ltd.

MODULE 4   POULTRY HEALTH MANAGEMENT, DISEASES AND THEIR EFFECTS

Unit 1   Health Management Practices in Poultry
Unit 2   Diseases of Poultry
Unit 3   Nutritional Diseases of Poultry
Unit 4   Economic Implication of Diseases of Poultry

UNIT 1   HEALTH MANAGEMENT PRACTICES IN POULTRY

CONTENTS

1.0   Introduction
2.0   Objectives
3.0   Main Content
       3.1   Farm management Practices and Hygiene
             3.1.1   Consultation
             3.1.2   Sources of Chicks
             3.1.3   Rearing of Poultry
             3.1.4   Brooding
             3.1.5   Ventilation
             3.1.6   Restriction
             3.1.7   Feeds and Feeding
                     Post-Mortem
             3.1.8   Examination
             3.1.9   Record Keeping
             3.1.10 Disposal of Dead Birds

Other Management
3.1.11 Steps
3.2   Prophylaxis
3.3   Vaccination in Poultry
4.0   Conclusion
5.0   Summary
6.0   Assignment
7.0   References

1.0   INTRODUCTION

For many years, the poultry industry has emerged as a major source of the much required animal protein. One major concern of the poultry farmer is the curtailment of mortalities in his flock. This is because attainment of impressive growth rate, high productivity and profit is closely related to overcoming the challenge of high mortalities. The productive life of poultry is relatively short (about 10 weeks for broiler chickens, 1-1½ years for commercial layers) and therefore any diseases
– induced defects to body and functions of birds virtually end up in irreparable damage to weight and egg production performances. It is very clear that poultry can ill-afford any recuperative period, no matter how short. Therefore the prevention of disease is the only good option and route to efficient productivity in poultry. Good management

practices that are easily adopted have been evolved as one of the tools to help whosoever keeps poultry to have a healthy stock in order to achieve his production objective(s). Other tools are preventive medication and vaccination. This unit seeks to highlight these tools.

2.0 OBJECTIVES

At the end of this unit, you should be able to:

- state the general principles of an effective health programme
- explain the possibility of modifying the general principles of an effective health programme to suit farm peculiarities
- explain the role of farm management practices, medication and vaccination to ensure both maximum profitability and productivity.

3.0 MAIN CONTENT

3.1 Farm Management Practices and Hygiene

Farm management practices show the general principles for disease prevention and efficient productivity in the stock. Hygiene on the other hand is the functional (day to day or periodic) component for achieving efficiency in disease control. The challenges caused by diseases are particularly important when birds are housed under intensive conditions with birds in close proximity to each other as it obtains in the modern poultry. This allows the maximum opportunity for diseases to spread from one bird to another. However, it should be noted also that even under extensive conditions birds can easily spread disease because they are normally housed close together at night in order to protect them from thieves and carnivorous animals. The following are important hygiene and farm management steps to ensure that disease attack and spread are minimized:

3.1.1 Consultation

Often, the poultry farmers who experience serious disease problems are those who fail to consult with the professionals whose opinions and advice are cogent. These are:

- The poultry extension specialist.
- The poultry pathologist.
- .The veterinarian.

Consultation with these specialists will help to prevent some of the common pitfalls and this should be done at the planning stage. Thespecialists will advise on various management practices to prevent diseases. These include:

1. Choosing a favourable geographical location to site the farm putting into consideration the production objectives.
2. Building design which involves the orientation of poultry buildings, spacing, animal comfort, ease of cleaning.
3. The types of feed for each category and mode of feeding.
4. The types of litter material available for use in deep litter house, depth of litter, litter hygiene and disposal.
5. Brooding of chicks and ventilation for adult stock
6. The control of vermins.
7. The control of human traffic both staff and visitors, hygiene of staff.
8. Culling operations.
9. How to handle disease outbreaks, early detection of diseases, veterinary services available, cleaning out.
10. How to eliminate stress factors by following high standards of management and hygiene.

3.1.2 Sources of Chicks

The source of chicks is an important aspect of management if you do not hatch eggs on your farm. Chicks and preferably day-old should be purchased from a reputable hatchery or a proven source. Many poultry diseases originate from the hatcheries while some are transmitted from the hen to the chicks through the egg. A good hatchery must therefore maintain a high level of sanitation to prevent chicks becoming infected.

3.1.3 Rearing of Poultry

The birds should be reared in separate houses according to their age groups and species. If birds of different ages and of different species are housed together, the spread of disease is encouraged. If birds of one age only are kept on one site there is far less chance of disease spreading from older birds to younger ones. This can be achieved if the poultry breeder follows the all-in/all out system. In this system, whether egg-type or meat-type, all the birds are brought onto the site at the same time and same age. At the end of the production period, all birds are removed, the manure is cleaned out, the houses thoroughly disinfected and a gap of at least two weeks is left between the selling of one batch of birds and the replacement with a new batch.

3.1.4 Brooding

Brooding is the care of baby chicks during the periods when supplementary heat is provided for the comfort of the birds. Duration of brooding has already been discussed in module 3 unit 1. Proper brooding is very important in preventing disease in chicks and minimizing loss.

3.1.5 Ventilation

In tropical climate, heat stress is probably the most important factor to contend with in poultry house designs. Poultry houses should be designed to provide adequate ventilation prevent excess dust and wet litter which can lead to ammonia build-up. Improper ventilation may cause wet-litter which in turn promotes development of coccidal oocyst. Coccidiosis is a very common disease of poultry especially when they are raised on deep litter system. Coccidial oocyst requires moisture to develop into the infective stage. Proper ventilation promotes dry litter and therefore inhibits the development of coccidial oocyst, thus preventing coccidiosis. Poor ventilation on the other hand promotes rapid spread of poultry diseases especially those that can easily spread from bird to bird through the air.

3.1.6 Restriction

Non-workers in the farm should be restricted from entering the flock house. This is a good way of preventing introduction of diseases from outside to the farm. Where it is necessary to allow visitors on the farm, proper sanitary precautions must be taken to ensure they do not bring in disease to the flock. Vehicles and poultry equipment that have been used elsewhere are other ways by which diseases can be introduced into your farm. Such equipment and vehicles should be disinfected properly before use on the farm. Provide footbath containing a disinfectant at the entrance to each pen house. Prepare fresh disinfectant daily.

3.1.7 Feeds and Feeding

Adequate feeding together with other management steps is very essential for maintenance of flock health and productivity. Correct feeding is required for normal growth, vigour, egg production, hatchability and long productive life. Poultry feed rations are formulated to contain all the nutrients essential for the proper functioning of the body in right quantities. Deficiency of any of these essential nutrients often times causes disease conditions. Water is the cheapest of all the feed nutrients and the supply must be tested for quality to make it safe for poultry. Poultry feeds should be purchased from a reputable feed manufacturer. It is good to seek for advice from older farmers in your locality on the brands of feed available. A good feed kept for too long in the store may lose some of its essential nutrients. Also, the use of mouldy feeds results in aspergillosis or brooder pneumonia. Many poultry diseases can be spread through the faeces containing the feeders and waterers. Therefore, feeders and waterers must be designed in a way that prevents faecal contamination.

3.1.8 Post-Mortem Examination

With the best of management, occasional loss is experienced as a result of death of known and unknown causes. Efforts should be made to find out the cause of death even with a loss of one bird with a view to preventing recurrence. One way of determining the cause of death is post-mortem examination which veterinary services will provide. Whenever a bird is found dead, it should be removed at once for examination before it is disposed off. Freshly killed or dead animal is the most suitable for a post-mortem examination but if veterinary services are not readily available, then the dead bird can be kept in a refrigerator for some days. The veterinary doctor based on his findings will then give professional advices on the steps to take to prevent future occurrence.

3.1.9 Record Keeping

Record keeping is very important as it helps to give the required warning of an impending problem. Most disease problems are reflected in the feeding pattern of the birds. A drop in feed consumption is usually one of the first signs exhibited by a sick bird. There are three types of record that all poultry farmers should keep, namely:

1. Inventory record
2. Production record
3. Financial record

Among these three, production record is the one that relates very closely to poultry health management.

3.1.10 Disposal of Dead Birds

One way of preventing the spread of disease from dead birds is by proper disposal of the dead ones. For this reason, dead birds must be buried or burnt immediately. Vermins may serve as carriers of disease germs after contacting diseased or dead birds. The essential management procedures to minimize or prevent the spread of diseases from dead birds are as follows:

1.   Immediate removal of all dead birds from cages, floor pens.

2.   Keeping the waste bin for holding dead birds closed always to prevent contact by flies, dogs, insects, etc.
3.   The waste bins should be well isolated from the operational areas.
4.   After handling a dead bird, all equipment, and materials used should be disinfected.

Methods of disposal vary and a farmer should adopt whichever method he considers suitable for his needs. The common methods are:

1.   **Incineration:** This involves burning of the carcasses completely until ash is formed. The incinerator is the place where the burning is done.
2.   **The Disposal Pit:** This uses continuous bacterial action to break down the soft tissues as dead birds are added. Pits are constructed in the ground to deposit dead birds.
3.   **Rendering:** This helps to recycle dead birds by converting dead carcasses into animal by- product and feed.
4.   **Acid Hydrolysis:** This uses phosphoric acid, water and heat to convert indigestible animal tissues into a high-protein feed supplement. Carcasses are ground and then hydrolysed by the acid and blended directly into a feed formulation. The hydrolysis plant is expensive and is not for small scale poultry operation.

3.1.11 Other Important Management Steps

1.   Stock the house bearing in mind the feeding and drinking space, and bird space requirement. The stocking density or ratio must not be ignored.
2.   Keep vermins out of the poultry house-since these have been shown to have the capacity to introduce micro-organisms into poultry house.

3. Feed troughs and water troughs should be cleaned out daily and refilled with fresh feed and fresh and cool drinking water. Stale
    feed and water are veritable media for the growth of micro-organisms.
4. Make use of veterinary services before medication and vaccination administration for proper guidance and effectiveness.
5   Sick birds should be isolated promptly from the flock. The farmer should not hesitate to destroy them by burying them or burning them in an incinerator. To be able to detect sick birds, the farmer must observe the flock at regular intervals.

3.2   Prophylaxis

This is the prevention of a disease. It has been found that the most careful observance of good farm management and hygiene practices may not be full-proof in the prevention of diseases. Occasions for additional efforts will arise. However such occasions can be greatly minimized by the use of preventive medication and vaccines. It is important to know why and when to employ preventive medication and vaccines. For instance:

1. When it is known that certain diseases are endemic in an area and therefore pose a threat which can only be handled by preventive medication and or vaccination e.g. Newcastle disease, fowl pox, Gumboro disease, Marek's Coccidiosis
2. When unfavourale climatic changes are likely to precipitate a disease condition like coryza in poultry
3. When stock density or litter management problems raise the possibility of disease outbreak like coccidiosis.

In these and other instances, vaccines or drugs can be strategically applied to pre-empt disease outbreak. Since timing of disease out break cannot be predicted with regular precision, this has given rise to routine vaccination and medication practices in farm animals including poultry. The vaccines or coccidiostats are applied when the disease has not appeared in stock, so that defensive mechanisms are introduced through the development of antibodies in the one case and the destruction of the early stages of the disease agent (coccidia) in the other. Different coccidiostats should not be mixed since it may be harmful. Coccidiostats should be mixed in the food but should be withdrawn four days before the birds are slaughtered so that it does not find its way through poultry meat into the consumer. Amprolium is a potent coccidiostat to treat birds when an outbreak of coccidiosis occurs in a flock.

3.3   Vaccination in Poultry

This is the process of vaccine administration in chickens to protect them against bacterial and viral diseases of economic importance by stimulating immunity in the chickens. For vaccines to be used, they must be germ free and the chickens to be administered should be healthy. Vaccination is better than cure and has no alternative. The use of vitamins five days prior to vaccination date will help in reducing vaccination stress.

There are two types of vaccines in use:

1.	Live vaccine and
2.	Dead vaccine.

The live vaccine should precede the use of a dead vaccine. A typical vaccination schedule is presented in Table 3.5.

Table 3.5: Vaccination Schedule for Poultry Farmers

Age	Type of Vaccine	Disease	Route
1 day	Newcastle disease Vaccine (1st dose)	Newcastle (ND)	Intra ocular (1/0)
2 weeks	Gumboro disease Vaccine (1st dose)	Gumboro	i/o, oral, i/m
3 weeks	Newcastle disease Vaccine-lasota (2$_{nd}$ dose)	Newcastle (ND)	Aerosol (air spray), oral, i/m.
5 weeks	Gumboro disease Vaccine (2$_{nd}$ dose)	Gumboro	i/o, oral, i/m
6-8 weeks	Fowl pox	Fowl pox	Wing web stab
7-8 weeks	Fowl typhoid/fowl Cholera vaccine	Fowl typhoid/fowl cholera	Subcutaneously (sc)
16-18 weeks	Newcastle disease (3$_{rd}$ dose)	Newcastle disease Lasota and komorov strain	Sc
30 weeks	Newcastle disease Disease vaccine	ND- lasota strain	oral

# 4.0	CONCLUSION

The poultry farmer needs certain tools to minimize mortality in his flock. The adoption of these tools namely good management practices, preventive medication and vaccination is imperative to have a healthy stock in order to achieve production objectives.

5.0 SUMMARY

This unit teaches the following:

- The importance of farm management and hygiene, steps to minimize the attack and spread of poultry diseases

- The difference between farm management and hygiene
- Prophylaxis, which is the prevention of disease
- Vaccination in poultry.

6.0 ASSIGNMENT

1. Mention the tools required by a poultry farmer to curtail losses of birds on the farm.
2. Mention the professionals whose services are needed for a successful poultry farm operation.
3. Enumerate the kind of advice you would expect the professionals to give.
4. Make a list of the farm management and hygiene steps to minimize disease problems on a poultry farm.
5. What role does the source of chicks play in poultry disease control?
6. Why would you restrict the entry of non-workers on the poultry farm?
7. How many times would you give gumboro vaccine to a batch of broilers?

7.0 REFERENCES/FURTHER READINGS

AERLS, (1986). *Poultry Farmer's Handbook of Disease Prevention.* Extension Bulletin No. 28. Poultry Series No. 3. AERLS, ABU Zaria. Nigeria.

Smith, A. J. (1990). *Poultry. The Tropical Agriculturist.* London & Basingstoke: Macmillan Education Ltd.

Usman, S.B. and Manasa, Y.S. (2002). *Poultry Made Easy*. Vom, Nigeria: National Veterinary Research Institute Printing Press.

UNIT 2   DISEASES OF POULTRY

CONTENTS

1.0   Introductio n
2.0   Objectives
3.0   Main Content
    3.1   Viral Diseases of Poultry
        3.1.1 Newcastle Disease/Ranikhet Diseases
        3.1.2 Fowl Pox
        3.1.3 Gumboro Disease (Infectious Bursal Disease)
        3.1.4 Marek's Disease
        3.1.5 Avian Encephalmelitis (Epidemic Tremor)
    3.2   Bacterial Diseases of Poultry
        3.2.1 Pollorum Disease (Bacillary white Diarrhoea)
        3.2.2 Fowl Typhoid
        3.2.3 Fowl Cholera (Pasteurellosis)
                Chronic Respiratory Disease (Avian
        3.2.4 Mycoplasma)
        3.2.5 Infectious Coryza
    3.3   Fungal Diseases of Poultry
        3.3.1 Aspergillosis (Brooder Pneumonia)
        3.3.2 Favus
    3.4   Parasitic Diseases of Poultry
        3.4.1 Coccidiosis
        3.4.2 Ascariosis
        3.4.3 Syngamosis
        3.4.4 Tapeworm Infection
        3.4.5 Lice Infection
        3.4.6 Tick Infection
        3.4.7 Mite Infection
4.0   Conclusion
5.0   Summary
6.0   Assignment
7.0   References

1.0   INTRODUCTION

A disease is an unhealthy or abnormal physical state and/or appearance. It can be caused by living organisms (infectious agents) or faulty environments due to poor management. Chickens, like human beings are subjected to many diseases and parasites. There are even some poultry diseases with the same names like cholera, pox, typhoid, hepatitis etc. Chickens are also known to suffer from internal and external parasites. Some poultry diseases and parasites can be prevented while others cannot be prevented. Some cannot be controlled and cause death when contracted; others can be isolated and controlled. Some are present in the country and others are from foreign sources. Unless diseases and parasites are accurately identified and prevented or controlled, they can cause huge losses of chickens and consequently loss of money. In Nigeria, a conservative estimate shows that about 10 to 20% of the chickens produced die each year and diseases are the most important cause of the losses. The key is to prevent rather than to control. Poultry farmers need to be familiar with the causes and symptoms of the various common poultry diseases in order to plan an effective control programme. Poultry diseases can be classified under the following headings:

1. Viral diseases
2. Bacterial diseases
3. Fungal diseases
4. Parasitic and diseases
5. Nutritional diseases

The viral, bacterial, fungal and parasitic poultry diseases will be the focus of this unit and the nutritional diseases will be the focus of Unit 3 in this module.

2.0 OBJECTIVES

You are expected to be able to:

- describe common poultry diseases and parasites, and appropriate preventive or control measures
- distinguish unhealthy chickens from healthy ones.

3.0 MAIN CONTENT

3.1 Viral Diseases of Poultry

These are poultry diseases caused by virus. Some examples include Newcastle disease, fowl pox, leucosis complex, avian encephalomyelitis.

3.1.1 Newcastle Disease/Ranikhet Disease

It is a highly infectious and fatal viral disease. It attacks poultry of all ages. It is widely feared by those raising chickens world wide. When it occurs, the mortality rate can be as high as 100% in young chickens but lower in adult birds. The virus is transmitted through contact by chickens and other birds.

Symptoms – The most obvious symptom is a sudden high number of deaths. Other symptoms are nervousness, incoordination and paralysis; respiratory distress (coughing, gasping for air, wheezing); greenish diarrhea with fowl odour; drooping head, inactivity, and drowsiness; distended crop; eventually, death. In adult laying birds, symptoms may be loss of appetite, decreased water consumption and a rapid drop in egg production.

Control – Vaccinate chicks of one day against it and re-vaccinate again at 6 to 8 weeks. Newcastle disease is preventable by vaccination.

Treatment – There is no treatment for this disease once the outbreak occurs. Affected birds should be isolated and destroyed immediately. Antibiotics may be administered for 3 to 5 days to prevent bacterial infections.

3.1.2 Fowl Pox

This disease is very prevalent mostly among extensively managed flocks. It affects poultry of all ages especially growers and adults. The virus is very hardy and can remain viable in scabs for up to ten years. It is mechanically transmitted by mosquitoes and other blood sucking arthropods from infected birds to other birds. Birds can also become infected by ingesting an infective scab. Fowl pox manifests in two forms: the wet form which affects the mouth, oesophagus, trachea and pharynx, and the dry form which affects the skin (mostly the hairless sites like combs and wattles, face and the feet). The wet form is more serious than the dry form, causing high mortality.

Symptoms – The eyes, beak, comb and head will be covered with scabs and/or swellings. In the wet form, nodules are present in the mouth, along the digestive and respiratory tracts.

Control – Vaccination is the most reliable method of preventing fowl pox and this is done by the hatcheries.

Treatment – There is no drug to use when there is an outbreak. Treating the dry form is easier than the wet form. It involves scrapping the warts and cleaning the surface with disinfectant. When a few birds are affected, isolate them and use tincture of iodine to dab the raw bleeding surface. Administration of antibiotic to combat secondary bacterial infection and environmental stress is appropriate. Affected birds can also be destroyed.

3.1.3 Gumboro Disease (Infectious Bursal Disease)

It is a highly contagious viral disease affecting young chicks (3 to 6 weeks) with attendant grave economic losses.

Symptoms – Affected birds produce white watery droppings; have soiled vent feathers, ruffled feathers. Other symptoms are loss of appetite, vent pecking, reluctance to move and death.

Control – Vaccines are now available as a preventive measure.

Treatment – There is no known effective treatment. However increased ventilation is recommended with antibiotic medication.

3.1.4 Marek's Disease

This is a viral disease affecting mostly birds between 6 to 26 weeks of age. The virus is spread from an infected chicken to a n on-infected one through the air, poultry dust, by contact, sometimes faeces.

Symptoms – these include lameness or paralysis of the legs, droopy wings, blindness, poor respiratory rate and death of 10-30% of the flock.

Control – prevention of Marek's disease is by vaccination by the hatcheries at day old. Also procure genetically resistant chicks and main high sanitation standards.

Treatment – There is no treatment, thus affected chickens should be destroyed.

3.1.5 Avian Encephalomyelitis (Epidemic Tremor)

This viral disease affects all ages of chickens with mortality as high as 50%. Mostly chicks from day old to about 4 weeks of age are affected. This disease may symptomatically be confused with Newcastle disease. It is transmitted by chicken eating infected feed and litter materials. It can also come through eggs laid and hatched from infected stock.

Symptoms – Affected chicks have ataxia (lack of coordination of the leg muscles). The chickens cannot walk, lose muscle control and are paralyzed. First signs are shivering of the muscles, head, neck and legs. Death follows after a few days due to starvation and thirst.

Control – The chickens are vaccinated at the hatcheries before dispatching.

Treatment – No treatment is available. Affected chickens should be isolated and destroyed.

3.2 Bacterial Diseases of Poultry

These are poultry diseases caused by bacteria. Some examples are pullorum disease, fowl typhoid, fowl cholera, chronic respiratory disease etc.

3.2.1 Pullorum Disease (Bacillary white Diarrhoea)

This disease is caused by a bacterium called Salmonella pullorum. It causes high mortality in young chicks or poults and sporadic deaths in adults. The bacterium is present in the eggs and faeces of infected layers, infected chicks in the hatchery.

Symptoms – Affected chicks are weak, huddle together, droopy, suffer from diarrhea and remain sitting or standing for a long time in the same position. They produce chalk-white faeces which is the reason why it is called bacillary white diarrhea. This death rate in chicks is high

.

Control – Breeder flocks should undergo blood test to remove carriers and thereby ensure that hatching eggs and chicks are disease free. High level of sanitation must be maintained at the hatcheries. Incubators must be cleaned and fumigated after hatching. The best way to avoid the disease is to buy only chicks certified to be free from salmonella.

Treatment – Sulphur drugs like furazoloidone have been used successfully in treatment to reduce mortality only.

3.2.2 Fowl Typhoid

It is caused by a bacterium Salmonella gallinarum. The disease affects mostly adult chicken and in some cases turkeys

.

Symptoms – In the acute form, the comb and wattles of birds are congested and sudden death occurs. At the chronic stage, there are symptoms like anaemia, pale and shrunken combs and wattles, yellowish diarrhea, lack appetitie, listlessness and intense thirst.

Control – Sulphur drugs like furazolidone are available for use.

Treatment – Furazolidone is effective for treatment.

3.2.3 Fowl Cholera (Pasteurellosis)

This is a bacterial disease which is both infectious and contagious. It causes a high mortality in both chickens and in ducks. Mortality is low if it is the localized form but its high of it is septicaemia. The disease is caused by bacterial Pastenrella multocida or Pasteurella septica

Symptoms – These are greenish-yellow diarrhea, enlarged hot swollen combs and wattles, nasal discharges and difficulty in breathing, reduced appetite and weight loss.

Control – An annual vaccination of all birds with a live vaccine may prevent the disease.

Treatment – This is by application of intramuscular injections of terramycin or streptomycin. Infected birds should be removed, the litter changed and equipment and poultry house properly disinfected.

3.2.4 Chronic Respiratory Disease (Avian Mycoplasma)

This is an infectious disease of poultry caused by Mycoplasma spp. It affects both chicken and turkey. The disease is commonly referred to as CRD or air sac infection; It is normally a secondary infection following either parasitic or microbial infections or possibly after a stress factor.

Symptoms – These are manifested as respiratory signs. The first sign observed is a mild cough. The respiratory tracts and air sacs of the lungs are normally inflamed and may be filled with exudates. Mortality is low unless secondary infection occurs. Mortality is high in broilers and egg production may fall in layers.

Control – All affected birds should be destroyed. Equipment and poultry houses should be disinfected. Breeding flocks should be vaccinated to prevent the disease from being transmitted through eggs. Replacements should be obtained from mycoplasma free stock (blood tested stock).

Treatment – Antibiotics of the tetracycline groups are available for treatment.

3.2.5 Infectious Coryza

This disease is caused by a bacterium Haemophilus gallinarum. It affects chickens about 6 weeks of age and older ones. It is a disease which affects the respiratory system. It is usually associated with cold, damp weather. It spreads among chickens through sneezing and coughing of infected chickens.

Symptoms – The characteristic symptoms are difficult breathing, eye and nasal discharge, some swellings on the eye and nostrils accompanied by sneezing.

Control – Feed chickens with medicated, balance rations.

Treatment – Antibiotics like aureomycin or terramycin can be added to the feed or drinking water.

3.3 Fungal Diseases of Poultry

These are poultry diseases caused by fungi e.g. aspergillosis, favus, mycotoxicosis.

3.3.1 Aspergillosis (Brooder Pneumonia)

This is an infectious disease of birds caused by Aspergillus fumigatus. It affects the lungs in chicks, air sacs in old chickens causing respiratory distress. Wet litter and mouldy feed are common sources of aspergillus infection. Infection may start from the penetration of the eggs by the fungus, and incubator contamination.

Symptoms – Noticeable symptoms are difficult breathing, dyspnea, loss of appetite, loss of weight.

Control – The most effective control of the disease is by eliminating the sources of infection like wet litter, mouldy feed, and poor hygiene at the hatcheries. House must be well cleaned and disinfected between broods. The house should be well ventilated.

Treatment – There is no cure for affected birds.

3.3.2 Favus

This fungal disease is caused by a fungus Achorion gallinae or Trichophyton gallinae. It is an infection of the superficial layer of the skin of birds especially comb and wattle.

Symptoms – While encrusted scabs develop on comb and wattles and it spreads to other parts of the body. The feathers fall out and break off.

Control – Maintain high hygienic standards.

Treatment – Isolate affected birds and treat by washing the scabs and applying ointments to the affected parts.

3.4   Parasitic Diseases of Poultry

Parasites, both internal and external are common in the tropics. Both have the capacity to weaken the bird and in certain cases may be a secondary host for other diseases. External parasites may cause considerable loss to the poultry. They irritate poultry and sometimes kill them. They cause discomfort due to irritation, loss of plumage gradually leads to deterioration in the health of the flock and reduction in egg production among layers or retarded growth among the young birds. The birds will be pre-occupied with scratching and do not feed well leading to poor performance. External parasites can also serve as rectors transmitting diseases from one bird to another. Besides the protozoan parasite Trichomonas gallinae in pigeons, the most important internal parasites in poultry are the helminthes. Some examples of parasitic diseases are coccidiosis, ascariosis, syngamosis tapeworm infection, lice infestation.

3.4.1 Coccidiosis

This disease of poultry is caused by a protozoan parasite which resides in the walls of the chicken's intestine and will cause death at any age. Coccidiosis is very common in Nigeria and is probably the biggest killer of chickens. It is said to be caused by 8 to 9 distinct species of porotozoa of the genus Eimeria. It is spread to chickens particularly up to the age of 12 weeks through contaminated food, water or litter. Each species of Eimeria attacks a different portion of the intestines or caeca and it is particularly prevalent in chickens that are kept intensively which have the maximum possibility of taking up the disease from their fellow chickens.

Symptoms – Droppings are watery and greenish or brown in colour often containing blood. The affected birds lose appetite, their feathers become ruffled and soiled. Combs are pale and they tend to huddle together in corners. Their heads pull back into their body with the eyes usually kept closed.

Control – Chickens should be fed with medicated (coccidiostat mixed feed) feed at all times. Keep the litter dry and loose and keep your chicks in thoroughly disinfected pens on their arrival. Coccidiostas like Amprolium or Deccox may be used as preventive drugs for the first 8 weeks. Prevent the faecal contamination of the feed and the drinking water. The safest way to avoid coccidiosis is to raise chickens on wire floors where the faeces are passed out of reach.

Treatment – Add to the drinking water a coccidiostat. Isolate sick birds and when the attack dies down disinfect litter and sterilise pens.

3.4.2 Ascariosis

This disease is caused by Ascaridia galli (round worms) which is common among local chicken and other poultry species which are not well managed. The round worms occupy the small intestine, are white or whitish yellow and 2.5-10cm long. Te worms and eggs are frequently passed in droppings. The eggs develop into the infective stage in 10 to 12 day under favourable temperature and moisture conditions, hatch either in the proventriculus or in the duodenum. After hatching, the young larve line free in the lumen of the posterior duodenum for the first 9 days, and then penetrate the mucosa and cause haemorrhages.

Symptoms – The most observed symptom is cattaarhal or haemorhogical enteritis among young birds. Adults are usually symptom
– less except loss of conditions. Worms can also be observed in droppings. There could also be persistent diarrhoea.

Control – Young and adult flocks should not be reared in the same house.

Treatment – Administer piperazine to the birds and also treat the deep litter with same drug, once in too months. Furthermore, maintain high hygienic standards.

3.4.3 Syngamosis

This disease is caused by a parasite Syngamus trachea (gape worm) which uses earthworm as a transport host. The worm is found in the lower part of the windpipe and sometimes in smaller air passages of fowls usually not less than 6 weeks of age.

Symptoms – Affected birds often shake their heads and gasping for air. Death also results from suffocation.

Control – This is by maintaining good hygienic condition of poultry unit and destruction of the transport host.

Treatment – Infected birds can be treated with anthelminths like thiabendazole.

3.4.4 Tapeworm Infection

The most common and economically important tapeworms (cestodes) are Darainea proglothina, Raillietina spp., Amoebotaenia spencides and Choamotaenia infundibulum. Part of the life cycle of these worms occurs in intermediate hosts such as snails and earthworms, which when eaten by fowls expose them, to infection.

Symptoms – These are usually observed among young birds and include loss of appetite, droopiness, thirst and emaciation.

Control – The intermediate hosts should be attacked by the use of molluscides and insecticides.

Treatment – Infected chicken should be treated with anthelminths. Also a good hygienic environment should be maintained.

3.4.5 Lice Infection

Lice are the most common external parasite. Lice differ from mites and ticks because they spend their entire life cycle on the body of the bird. There are two types of lice attacking animals namely blood sucking and biting lice. Only the biting lice attack chickens and can be found at different locations on the body of the fowl. Lice are three types:

1. Body lice which are found around the vent and tail.
2. Head lice which are found around the head and neck regions
3. Shaft lice which are found around the shaft of the feathers.

Lice reproduce rapidly at about 30,000 per female and can live up to 3 months. They spread by direct contact and die once they leave the chickens. They are about 3mm long, oral shaped and grey or yellow in color.

Symptoms – General ill health, constant irritation, scabs, ruffled feathers, slow weight gain, decreased egg production and death in some smaller chickens.

Control – The birds should be inspected regularly for presence of any external parasite. Prevent overcrowding and poor hygiene. The nests should be kept clean and if the birds roost at night, perches should be painted with nicotine sulphate, and creosote placed in the cracks and joints of the roost.

Treatment – This can be achieved by spraying the birds with malathion solution or by dusting individual chicken with pyrethrinsor malathion powder. In the case of deep litter systems, the litter and all equipment except the feeders and waterers should be sprayed and dusted.

3.4.6 Tick Infection

Ticks are blood sucking organisms and are in various forms mainly flat, egg-shaped, disc shaped. They also carry diseases such as spirochetosis. They are normally found in hot dry areas and they spend part of their life cycle in cracks in walls and roofs and in other equipment made of word.

Symptoms – These are loss of appetite and weight, and possibly anaemia.

Control – Keep equipment clean and avoid the use of wood in equipment such as feeders and nesting box. Also avoid crevices in the poultry houses where ticks can hide.

Treatment – This can be done by spraying the birds with malathion solution or by dusting the chicken with pyrethrins or malathion powder as in lice.

3.4.7 Mite Infection

Mites are very small and almost invisible. There are many known species. Some stay on the chickens while others attack only at night and hide in the woodwork and litter during the day.

Symptoms – Symptoms are specific to species of mites. Scaly leg mites make the birds lame, and the legs swell, appear scaly and encrusted. Red mites are nocturnal. They cause loss of weight and decrease in egg production, and may cause anaemia. Dephiming mites attack the base of feathers and birds pull out their feathers to relieve itching, hence their name.

Control – This is the same as for ticks.

Treatment – There is no treatment for the scaly leg mite except for culling infected birds. For other mites the treat is the same as for lice and ticks.

4.0   CONCLUSION

In this unit, you have been introduced to the diseases of poultry, their causes, symptoms, effects, prevention and treatments where applicable with a view to showing the importance of prevention of diseases.

5.0   SUMMARY

This unit has taught:

- The classification of poultry diseases
- Some examples of diseases in the viral, bacterial, fungal and parasitic classes
- The symptoms, prevention and treatment of the viral, bacterial, fungal and parasitic diseases of poultry.

6.0   ASSIGNMENT

1.   Make a list of the classes of poultry diseases.
2.   Give two examples in each of the classes.
3.   Describe the symptoms, prevention, and treatment of gumboro, fowl typhoid, aspergillosis and tapeworm infection.

7.0   REFERENCES

Banerjee, G.C. (1976). *Poultry*. (3rd ed). New Delhi: Oxford and IBH Publishing Co. PVT. Ltd.

Oluyemi, T. A. and Roberts, F.A. (1981). *Poultry Production in Warm Wet Climates*. Ibadan: Spectrum Books Ltd

UNIT 3   NUTRITIONAL DISEASES OF POULTRY

CONTENTS

1.0   Introduction
2.0   Objectives
3.0   Main Content
    3.1   Causes of Dietary Inadequacies
    3.2   Nutrient constituents of Poultry Feed, and Disorders and Diseases
       3.2.1 Carbohydrate
       3.2.2 Fats
           Protein
       3.2.3 s
       3.2.4 Minerals and Vitamins
           3.2.4.1 Vitamin A Deficiency
           3.2.4.2 Rickets
           3.2.4.3 Encephalomalacia (Crazy Chick Disease)
           3.2.4.4 Curled-toe Paralysis
           3.2.4.5 Chick Dermatitis
           3.2.4.6 Slipped Tendon (Perosis)
       3.2.5 Water
4.0   Conclusion
5.0   Summary
6.0   Assignment
7.0   References

1.0 INTRODUCTION

The modern poultry industry has evolved from decades of systematic growth and scientific innovations. Hence, today you can see a standard commercial egg laying bird laying almost ten times the number and twice the size of eggs laid by her ancestor decades ago. This and other improvements associated with the modern poultry bird are the outcome of genetic selection, which are in turn dependent on management and husbandry inputs such as nutrition, housing and health. An important feature of modern poultry birds is movement restriction because they are housed. Therefore the birds are entirely dependent on the operator to provide an adequate diet to meet their nutritional requirements for good health and efficiency in products formation. For a diet to be adequate it must supply these elements not only in sufficient quantities but also in the right proportions. Proper nutrition therefore, is a pre-requisite to a profitable poultry operation. Essential nutrients are required not only for normal growth and performance, their absence results in deficiency diseases.

2.0   OBJECTIVES

You are expected to be able to describe:

- the types of nutritional diseases of poultry as a consequence of dietary inadequacies
- how dietary inadequacies occur and
- how to prevent these inadequacies.

3.0   MAIN CONTENT

3.1   Causes of Dietary Inadequacies

Nutritional problems in poultry can be as a result of one or more of the following factors:

1.   Absence of specific nutritional element(s) in feeds and feed stuffs
2.   Insufficiency of nutritional element(s) in feeds and feedstuffs
3.   Excess of nutritional element(s) in feeds and feedstuffs
4.   Denaturation of nutrient(s) in feeds and feedstuffs in the cause of processing
5.   Imbalance of nutrient(s) in formulated and compounded feed(s)
6.   Bio-unavailability of nutritional element(s) in compounded feeds
7.   Starvation in experimental situations or inadequate feed intake
8.   Dysfunction of the digestive system and associated organs as a result of disease.

3.2   Nutrient Constituents of Poultry Feed and Disorders and Diseases

The poultry diet contains six nutrients namely: carbohydrates, proteins, fats, minerals, vitamins and water. However, the bulk of the feed is carbohydrate, protein and some fats. The minerals and vitamins are present in minute quantities while the moisture content depends on the kind of processing feedstuffs are subjected to.

3.2.1 Carbohydrate

Carbohydrates supply most of the energy in poultry diet required for all its metabolic activities like growth, egg production, movements. Maize is one of the richest sources of energy and normally, only marginal deficiencies of carbohydrates can be noticed under field conditions.

Symptoms – Problems which can be fully or partly associated with carbohydrate deficiency are:
1.   Impairment of all metabolic functions.
2.   Reduced growth rate
3.   Poor feathering
4.   Reduction in number and size of eggs laid
5.   Reduced liveability.
5.   Mortalities.

Feeds with high energy content along with other nutritional deficiencies and environmental factors have been implicated in the causation of fatty liver syndrome (FLS) in layers. Furthermore, FLS and fatty liver and haemorrhagic kidney syndrome in broilers and growers should not be ignored when other energy feedstuffs are substituted for maize as source of energy.

Control – The metabolisable energy requirements of poultry at each physiological state must be used in diet formulation. In addition correct measurements of each of the feeding stuffs must be made when diets are being compounded.

3.2.2 Fats

Fats are good sources of energy and essential fatty acids like linoleic, linolenic and arachidonic acids in poultry diet. A lack or deficiency of these fatty acids will result in:

1.   Suboptimal growth.
2.   Fatty liver problems.
3.   Susceptibility to respiratory diseases.

When a feed goes rancid because of the oxidation of its unsaturated fatty acids, many vitamins are destroyed and the free amino groups or protein are bound thereby reducing their availability.

Control – Add antioxidant to feed and feeds should not be kept for more than 3 weeks in the store unfed to poultry.

3.2.3 Proteins

Proteins are sources of dietary amino acids needed by poultry for growth and productivity. There are about 20 amino acids, eleven of which are classified as essential amino acids (EAA). Deficiency symptoms caused by EAA are:

1. Reduced growth
2. Poor feathering
3. Lowered egg production
4. Reduction in egg size
5. Frizzled feathers (specific for arginine deficiency
6. Poor skin ad feather pigmentation (specific for lysine deficiency)
7. Stunted growth (specific for glycine)
8. Poor liveability
9. Higher mortality rates.

Control – In feed compounding, determined appropriate inclusion rates of protein feedstuffs like fish meal, blood meal, soyabean meal, groundnut cake meal etc according to feeding standards have to be adhered to.

3.2.4 Minerals and Vitamins

In performing their physiological functions, inter-relationships exist among many minerals and vitamins. Thus the nutritional problems they cause will be considered in this light.

3.2.4.1 Vitamin A Deficiency

Affected chicks have ruffled feathers, unthrifty, lack coordination, retarded growth, staggering gait and eye disorders. In adult birds there is a decline in egg production and hatchability. Prevention is by giving synthetic vitamin A preparation.

3.2.4.2 Rickets

This is a nutritional disorder due to deficiency or in balance of calcium, vitamin D or phosphorus. Rickets is mostly seen in young birds.

Symptoms – This characterized by abnormal skeletal development. Symptoms are soft bones and beak, retarded growth, thin-shelled eggs, poor egg production and hatchability, and abnormal gait, reduced appetite, reduced activity and sensitivity, and increased mortality.

Control – Rations containing adequate calcium, phosphorus and vitamin D should be given. Sun dried feds are useful.

3.2.4.3 Encephalomalacia (Crazy Chick Disease)

This is a disease of young chicks due to deficiency of vitamin E in the feed. Vitamin E is an unstable compound which is easily destroyed by unsaturated fatty acid. Also this disease may arise due to storing feed for an excessive long period resulting in loss of vitamin E.

Symptoms – The symptoms of the disease include in coordinated gait, head retraction, paralysis, prostration, somersaulting, sterility and reproductive failure, poor egg hatchability.

Control – compounded diets should not be kept (stored) for too long to prevent loss of vitamin E. Addition of selenium and antioxidants to diets is effective.

Treatment – There is no cure for affected chicks but rectification of dietary deficiency will prevent new cases.

3.2.4.4 Curled-Toe Paralysis

This is a nutritional disease of chicks and poults caused by the deficiency of vitamin B_2 (riboflavin).

Symptoms – Curling of toes of affected chicks and poults, retarded growth diarrhea and high mortality. In the adult birds, there is poor egg hatchability.

Control – Compounded diets should have vitamin B_2 supplement.

Treatment – Water soluble multivitamins should be administered in the drinking water.

3.2.4.5 Chick Dermatitis

This is a disease caused by the deficiency of biotin and pantothenic acid. Calcium pantothenate is usually added to rations for young stock and breeding stock. Biotin is usually sufficient in practical rations but occurrence of perosis in turkeys under commercial conditions suggests need for extra supplementation.

Symptoms – Cracks appear on the soles of the feet and toes of chicks usually at 3 to 4 weeks. Crust is seen at corners o mouth and on the eyelids causing the eyelids to stick together. Apart from these symptoms, deficiencies of biotin acid pantothenic acid also result in retarded growth, reduced egg hatchability.

3.2.4.6 Slipped Tendon (Perosis)

This nutritional disease can be due to the deficiency of choline, folic acid, calcium, phosphorus and manganese. Choline requirements are usually met in feedstuffs but may be supplemented in starter ration. Folic acid likewise is sufficient in common feedstuffs but may be supplemented for breeding chickens and turkeys.

Symptoms – There is a grass enlargement of the hock joint, birds are crippled and hock infection occurs.

Control – Addition of vitamin – mineral premixes to compounded diets is essential.

Treatment – Recovery is impossible especially after manifestation of symptoms.

3.2.4 Water

Water is described as a universal solvent. An interrelationship exists between feed and water in the performance of poultry.

Symptoms – In poultry, partial or total water deprivation will cause:

1. Lowered growth rate
2. Reduced egg production
3. Death as a result of dehydration.

Control – Drinking water should be provided *ad libitum*. Such water should be clean cool, and low in salts. For water from direct natural sources, it should be free from germs, agro-chemicals and industrial wastes developed economies where graded eggs attract a premium. In addition, some of the diseases associated with egg production problems also have the potential of causing other losses such as mortalities and stress.

4.0 CONCLUSION

In this unit, the nutritional diseases of poultry have been the subject for consideration. Thus the unit teaches the implication of the modern poultry birds viz a viz provision of adequate nutrition because of restriction of their movement.

5.0 SUMMARY

You are expected to have learnt the following:

- Causes of nutritional problems in poultry
- The nutrient constituents of poultry feed
- Nutritional diseases in poultry.

6.0 ASSIGNMENT

1. List causes of nutritional problems in poultry.
2. Enumerate the nutrients obtainable from poultry diets.
3. Mention the nutritional diseases you know.

7.0 REFERENCES/FURTHER READINGS

Banerjee, G.C. (1976). *Poultry*. (3rd ed). New Delhi: Oxford and IBH Publishing Co. PVT, Ltd.

Oluyemi, J. A. and Roberts, F.A. (1981). *Poultry Production in Warm Wet Climates*. Ibadan: Spectrum Books Ltd.

UNIT 4 ECONOMIC IMPLICATION OF DISEASES OF POULTRY

CONTENTS

1.0   Introduction
2.0   Objectives
3.0   Main Content
    3.1   Qualitative Analysis of the Economic Importance Diseases on the Poultry Industry
        3.1.1 Morbidity and/ Mortality
        3.1.2 Reduced Growth Rate
        3.1.3 Egg Production Problems
        3.1.4 Carcass Quality
        3.1.5 Public Health/Hazards
        3.1.6 Post-outbreak Cleanout
    3.2   Quantitative Analysis of Economic Impact of Disease on the Poultry Industry
4.0   Conclusion
5.0   Summary
6.0   Assignment
7.0   References

1.0   INTRODUCTION

Commercial poultry production as an enterprise enjoys a high degree of patronage in the livestock sub-sector of the agro-business in Nigeria. This is because there is no bias to its consumption, it has a short generation interval, very good genetic strains are available both for table meat and table egg, and also that it is uniquely amenable to skillful scientific manipulation for optimal yields and profits. In spite of all these seeming advantages of poultry over most other livestock species, it is considered generally as a risky, unpredictable, highly vulnerable and demanding enterprise not only by practitioners but also by those who perhaps have heard about the poultry production failures some farmers have experienced.

Loss due to diseases is one significant threat to a profitable poultry enterprise. Whereas, a farmer keeping a few birds on range at the backyard may not experience a devastating loss, a farmer raising multiples of hundred birds must as a matter of necessity maintain a healthy flock since the risk for diseases becomes increasingly high for him. The enormous challenge posed by poultry disease to achieving increased production is thus the thrust of this unit.

2.0   OBJECTIVES

You are expected to be able to:

- explain the severity of poultry diseases on the productivity of birds and profitability
- explain the need to put an effective health package in place in order to minimize the negative effect of diseases on poultry production.

3.0   MAIN CONTENT

3.1   Qualitative Analysis of the Economic Impact of Diseases on the Poultry Industry

One easily noticeable effect of disease outbreak in a poultry flock is the loss from mortality. It is important to note that there are diseases of poultry which may not be accompanied by mortality but which however cause significant economic losses through the following ways:

1.   High morbidity demanding treatment
2.   Reduced growth rate
3.   Egg production problems (lowered production, malformation and defects)
4.   Carcass quality
5.   Public health hazards
6.   Post-outbreak cleanout.

3.1.1 Morbidity and Mortality

The establishment of infection is often followed by clinical manifestations in a proportion (morbidity) of the affected flock. The proportion (morbidity) so affected varies according to the type of disease and it may or may not be followed by deaths (mortality) in the flock. It should be noted that, clinical manifestations alone without mortality would require therapeutic intervention at a cost to the farmer. The costs would include those for communication, diagnostic services, and purchase of drugs. When mortality occurs, then there is an added dimension to the losses incurred.

3.1.2 **Reduced Growth Rate**

Certain diseases are known not so much for the mortality which they cause as for their retardation of growth rate in poultry. This type of problem is of concern mostly when it involves broiler chicks. Growth retardation is especially critical to the production economy in broilers in which cost of extra feeding to attain expected market weight can be substantial. While, all diseases are generally capable of affecting growth rate at least to some extent, some diseases like CRD, mal-absorption syndrome are more specific in precipitating significant growth retardation in poultry.

3.1.3 Egg Production Problems

Some poultry disease as earlier mentioned in Module 4 Units 2 and 3 are known for their specific effects on eggs being laid. The effects could be quantitative like:

1. Delayed onset of lay
2. Delayed attainment of peak of production
3. Sub-optimal peak of egg lay
4. Variable drop in percent egg production
5. Cessation of egg production in individual birds
6. Reduction in size of egg
7. Shell defects and malformations
8. Watery egg white and yolk
9. It should be noted that the economic loss due to these problems is of major concern in the poultry industry.

3.1.4 **Carcass Quality**

Statutorily, poultry meat like other farm animal meat should be inspected to ascertain whether it is wholesome to be passed for human consumption. It should be noted that carcass or meat quality can be lowered appreciably by diseases like Marek's disease, infectious synovitis, sarcomas.

3.1.5 Public Health Hazards

Public health considerations include health risk from diseases of poultry which can be transmitted to farm workers, product processors and consumers. There have been some recent cases of continental and global bird epidemics which have caused deaths in humans as a result of contact with infected poultry. Other major examples of diseases in this category include salmonellosis and Newcastle disease.

3.1.6 Post -outbreak Cleanout

Consequent upon a disease outbreak, there is often the need to incur some extra cost on the following:

1.   Disposal of carcasses
2.   Disinfection of utensils and premises
3.   Replacement of litter
4.   New empty or unused space and
5.   Medication and revaccination.

These sources of extra costs may appear negligible, but they can add up to a very substantial economic loss in the event of frequent outbreaks.

3.2   Quantitative Analysis of Economic Impact of Disease on the Poultry Industry

In the evaluation of the quantitative analysis of the economic implication of poultry disease on poultry production, the appropriate thing should have been to tag specific cost-benefit to the relationship between poultry health and or disease, and poultry production. This is however difficult because of the following problems which confront a global reference and definite financial analysis of the losses attributable to disease in the poultry industry:

1.   Lack of unified standards for production targets
2.   Difficulty in defining health standards on a global scale
3.   Variable mortality allowance from place to place
4.   Veritable standards of inputs, drugs and vaccinations
5.   Variable prices of poultry products
6.   Lack of data from many countries or failure to report losses in many individual farms
7.   Lack of uniform classification of items that constitute direct or indirect losses
8.   Lack of an organized pool or centre for data collection.

These problems suggest that it may be easier and more feasible to restrict financial analysis to individual farms or cases than giving it a global approach.

4.0   CONCLUSION

This unit has considered the practical significance of diseases of poultry and how they affect profitability, the performance of birds and the health of consumers with a view to provoking the poultry farmer to guard seriously against disease outbreak on the farm.

5.0   SUMMARY

This unit teaches the following:

- That while some poultry diseases cause mortality, some do not but impact negatively on some indices
- The difference between mortality and morbidity
- The qualitative and quantitative effects of poultry diseases on the poultry industry
- The difficulties involved in making the quantitative analysis of the effect of poultry diseases.

6.0   ASSIGNMENT

1. State the other ways by which poultry diseases cause effects different from mortality.
2. Enumerate the factors which make the quantitative analysis of poultry diseases difficult.
3. What do you understand by a post-outbreak cleanout?
4. Mention at least two diseases which can lower the quality of a carcass or meat.

7.0   REFERENCES

Adene, D.F. (2004). *Poultry Health and Production Principles and Practices*. (1st ed). Ibadan: Sterling-Horden Publishers (Nig) Ltd.